"IT'S IMPOSSIBLE ... ... YA"*

"[Tonya] is a Larry Bird or Wayne Gretzky. She's the best there has ever been athletically. There is not another figure skater who has ever laced up skates who could hold her skates. She has more talent than God has ever given anybody."

—Larry McBride, owner,
Valley Ice Arena, Beaverton, Oregon
as quoted in *The Oregonian*

"Tonya eats, lives, breathes, sleeps because she wants skating. And if someone tells her she can't do it, she'll do it . . . better and better."

—LaVona Golden,
Tonya's mother

"Most girls needed to be talked into doing some of the hard things. Not Tonya. She'd try anything. She was fearless."

*—Antje Spethmann, skater
as quoted in *The Oregonian*

"People like her because she's a great skater, not because she's Tonya. She has an air about her that puts people off, an air of, 'If you don't like it, tough luck, that's me.' That's a hard way to make friends."

—David Webber,
father of one of Tonya's closest friends

THIN ICE
THE COMPLETE, UNCENSORED STORY OF TONYA HARDING

America's Bad Girl of Ice Skating

FRANK COFFEY and JOE LAYDEN

PINNACLE BOOKS
WINDSOR PUBLISHING CORP.

PINNACLE BOOKS are published by

Windsor Publishing Corp.
475 Park Avenue South
New York, NY 10016

The P logo Reg U.S. Pat & TM off. Pinnacle is a trademark of Windsor Publishing Corp.

First Printing: February, 1994

Printed in the United States of America

Photograph of Eugene Saunders appears in the photo section
courtesy of Doug Beghtel/*The Oregonian*/SYGMA Photos.

*This book is dedicated to Tony Seidl,
who accelerates from zero to 60 faster than
any man or woman in all of book publishing.*

ACKNOWLEDGMENTS

Those of us who work in publishing know that all books are created by group effort; the following people made valued contributions to a project executed under a challenging deadline. At Pinnacle Books we'd especially like to thank our talented editors, Paul Dinas and Ann LaFarge, publisher Walter Zacharius, publicity director Laura Shatzkin, and editorial assistant, Susan Lippe. Thanks also to Deborah Hartnett, John Pynchon Holms, Robert Engle and Sherry Tunkel, the finest canape purveyor in all of Manhattan.

—FC & JL

To my wife, Sue, whose patience and understanding allowed me to chase a dream. And to the Albany *Times Union*, for its support and encouragement.

—JL

To my brother Wayne—in this case the competition. I hope I'll be buying.

—FC

Tragedy:
a serious play having an unhappy or disastrous ending brought about by the characters or central character impelled, in ancient drama, by fate or, more recently, by moral weakness, psychological maladjustment or social pressures.
—*Webster's New World Dictionary*

"In skating over thin ice our safety is in our speed."

—Ralph Waldo Emerson

The Cast of Characters

TONYA HARDING: 23 years old. Born and raised in Portland, Oregon. Two-time U.S. national figure skating champion. Began skating when she was not quite four years old. Showed tremendous promise at an early age. Small (5' 1", 105 pounds), but very athletic, aggressive skater. First American woman ever to land a triple Axel in competition. Childhood was extremely difficult. Mother was allegedly abusive, father suffered from physical problems that often prevented him from working. Family had little money and stability—had eight different addresses in the Portland area while Harding was growing up. Married Jeff Gillooly in 1990, when she was 19 years old. Filed several complaints with police during their three-year marriage. Divorced Gillooly in summer of 1993, but reconciled shortly thereafter. Volatile personality and "rough edges" prevented her from landing many endorsements. Implicated in the attack on Nancy Kerrigan, but not charged.

Said she learned of the plot after it happened, but denied any prior knowledge.

NANCY KERRIGAN: 24 years old. Resident of Stoneham, Massachusetts. Assaulted on January 6 at Cobo Arena in Detroit following a practice session for the nationals. Named to U.S. Olympic team despite being unable to compete in nationals (which serve as Olympic Trials). Bronze medalist in 1992 Olympics. National champion in 1993. Had been skating particularly well in the months prior to her attack, and was favored to win at the nationals. Was, and is, a valuable endorsement commodity.

JEFF GILLOOLY: 26 years old. Allegedly masterminded the plot to assault Nancy Kerrigan. Portland resident. Graduated from David Douglas High School in 1985. Worked as a clothing store salesman and as a conveyor belt operator for the Oregon Liquor Control Commission. Married Tonya Harding in March, 1990. Theirs has been a stormy relationship, filled with passion and pain. They have separated on several occasions. Twice—in 1991 and 1993—Gillooly was the recipient of a restraining order barring him from coming near Harding. They divorced in the summer of 1993, reconciled a few months later. Described as a bit of a control freak by some. Tried, in 1992, to serve as Harding's coach, though he knew almost nothing about figure skating. The arrangement did not last.

SHAWN ERIC ECKARDT: 26 years old. Portland resident. Allegedly helped arrange the plot to assault Nancy Kerrigan. Described by virtually all who knew him as "a blowhard." A big man (320 pounds) with big dreams—fantasies, really. A computer hacker who lived with his parents and yet fancied himself a master of espionage and counter-terrorism. Tossed out such phrases as "asset-protection strategies." Résumé included such outrageous lies as "successfully tracked and targeted terrorist cells throughout the Middle East, Central America and Europe; coordinated and conducted successful hostage retrieval operations." According to the dates on the résumé, Eckardt accomplished these remarkable feats of bravery when he was between 16 and 20 years of age. A high school and community college dropout who liked to pretend that he could arrange protection or mayhem; that he could move illegal goods, including drugs, if necessary. Fascinated by guns and survivalism and wealth, and yet he ran his small business, World Bodyguard Services, Inc., out of his parents' house and drove a 1974 Mercury with missing hubcaps.

A boyhood chum of Jeff Gillooly.

SHANE MINOAKA STANT: 22 years old. The man who allegedly attacked Nancy Kerrigan. Born in Portland, spent time in California as a child, returned to Portland as a teenager.

Resident of Phoenix, where he lives with his uncle, Derrick Smith. A bounty hunter and survivalist. A rugged, sometimes hostile young man who carries 225 pounds on his 6-foot frame. Prominent scars on his face and head. Looked like a body-builder, which was precisely what he was. According to former classmates and acquaintances, Stant liked a good fight. Fascinated by violence. Arrested in 1991 for allegedly taking four cars from the parking lot of an auto dealership and going for a joyride. Spent 15 days in jail. Talked of becoming a bodyguard.

DERRICK BRIAN SMITH: Allegedly drove the getaway car for his nephew, Shane Stant. Overweight, balding, appears far older than his 29 years. Resident of Phoenix. Former resident of Corbett, Oregon, near Portland. Friend of Shawn Eckardt, with whom he shared an interest in paramilitary activities. Former night janitor who moved to Phoenix with the hope of setting up his own "anti-terrorist training academy." His home in Corbett, according to neighbors, was an exercise in paramilitary madness, with barbed wire and bent-tree boobytraps surrounding the property. Armed services veteran who frequently told acquaintances that he had done work for a Swiss company that specialized in counterterrorism.

LaVONA GOLDEN: Mother of Tonya Harding. Married six times, and has filed for divorce from her current husband, James Golden, whom she married when Tonya was 17 years old. Widely described "mother-from-hell" for her allegedly abusive behavior toward her daughter, defends herself as a strict but caring mother who gave her daughter "everything we had." A hardscrabble life. Lived in numerous homes and trailers. Hard-working waitress through the years, who often hand-sewed her daughter's costumes. Has reported she suffered abuse in some relationships.

One

Outside Cobo Arena, winter tightened its grip.

The snow fell hard and fast, enveloping downtown Detroit in a shroud of white. This was Thursday, January 6, 1994, and it was not a particularly nice day for a drive in the Motor City. It was not a particularly nice day for much of anything in the Midwest, where folks were reeling from the effects of what was shaping up as one of the nastier winters in recent history. Detroit's traffic slowed to a crawl; mass transit schedules were thrown hopelessly out of whack; pedestrians lowered their heads, leaned into the elements and cursed under their breath, the steam rising with their words in a feeble display of anger and rebellion. It was a cold day. A mean day.

Nevertheless, a few hundred people had gathered in the stands at Cobo to watch the final day of practice prior to the 1994 U.S. Figure Skating Association (USFSA) championships. They were zealots, mostly—little girls in pigtails who had been rising before dawn to work on their compulsories, and their parents, who had paid for lessons and skates and ice time and sequined outfits . . . plus an everpresent band of hardcore fans.

These were the people who truly understood the magnitude of this event, who could appreciate the dedication and sacrifice and pain that had gone into simply qualifying for the Olympic Trials. Maybe some of those little girls would make it themselves one day. Maybe. For now, though, they were content to watch, dreamily, as their idols cut up the ice. They cheered and applauded and begged for autographs.

Outside the storm raged on, but in here it was warm. In here it was another world, apart and separate, governed only by the rules of fair competition.

During the course of the week their jaws had dropped as they watched the likes of 23-year-old Tonya Harding of Portland, Oregon, Kerrigan's chief rival the past few years, and 13-year-old Michelle Kwan of Torrance, California perform their artistic wonders.

But their favorite—America's favorite—was Nancy Kerrigan. At once strong and elegant, the 24-year-old from Stoneham, Massachusetts, was the picture of athletic grace and beauty on the ice, yet soft-spoken, almost delicate, when distanced from competition. In fact, that delicacy had occasionally been a source of distress for Kerrigan in the past. After winning the nationals in 1993, she had fairly bombed at the world championships in Prague, finishing fifth when it was expected that she would contend for a gold medal.

Kerrigan was a bundle of nerves then, a world-class athlete suffering from a devastating case of performance anxiety. Oddly enough, coming off her victory in the nationals, she seemed to lack confidence. Even in the relative privacy of practice she would deliberately omit certain moves from her long program. Maybe she feared injury. Maybe she questioned her own talent. Whatever the motivation, whatever the source of the emotion, it was clear that Kerrigan was scared, and the result, predictably, was a hugely disappointing fifth-place finish.

On that day in March, after finishing her program and while awaiting the inevitable modest scores from the judges, Kerrigan broke into tears. "I just want to die," she said to her coaches, Evy Scotvold and his wife Mary. A microphone picked up the words and a national television audience swelled with sympathy.

Life had been better for Nancy Kerrigan since then, though. In the months following, she rededicated herself to the sport of figure

skating. She worked harder than ever. She
lifted more weights, skated longer and harder
in practice, increased her aerobic capabilities.
She enlisted the services of a sports psychologist—someone who, presumably, would be able
to peek into her mind and fortify her fragile
psyche.

The poor performance at the world championship trials notwithstanding, endorsement offers were flooding into the offices of Kerrigan's
agent, Jerry Solomon of ProServ. It was no surprise, really; she was, after all, a stunning
beauty, with a bright smile and high cheek-
bones that prompted some to label her "the
Katharine Hepburn of figure skating." Kerrigan turned down many of the offers, though.
She wanted to concentrate on skating. She
wanted to prove something to herself and to
the world.

"She's never worked this hard before," Kerrigan's longtime coach, Evy Scotvold, told *Sports
Illustrated* during the nationals. "She's never
done the run-throughs she's doing now. Double
run-throughs. Going for perfect run-throughs.
She's in fantastic shape. Her power is incred-
ible. When she skates she looks like she needs
a bigger ice surface."

The fear, apparently, was gone, the appre-
hension melted away. Kerrigan was poised to
defend her title and, more importantly, move

on to Lillehammer, Norway, site of the 1994 winter Olympics.

In Kerrigan's mind, that was the way it would work. Her fans envisioned the drama unfolding in similar fashion. And so they stood and cheered wildly when she skated onto the ice that afternoon in Detroit, looking so perfect, so feminine, so athletic, in a white lace dress and pearl earrings, her hair tugged back in a ponytail.

It was the first of two scheduled practice sessions for Kerrigan; a second was planned for 11:30 that evening. But because the weather was foul and the hour was late, Kerrigan fretted over the possibility of not getting back to Cobo for a second workout. She opted to stay late during the afternoon session; she was, in fact, the last skater to leave the ice.

For reasons that have not been adequately addressed, security at Cobo Arena that day was far from tight. Members of the media wore official press credentials and thus had access to most areas of the building. Unfortunately, so did just about everyone else. Fans and sociopaths alike could leave their seats high above the ice and stroll casually to the edge of the rink, where they could then stand an arm's length from the object of their affection—or their disdain—for several minutes at a time.

Eventually, a security guard or usher would come along and shoo them away, but in the meantime they would get their brush with fame, their glimpse of stardom.

"You could walk through anywhere without showing a badge," noted Frank Carroll, Michelle Kwan's coach. That observation was supported by *San Francisco Examiner* columnist Joan Ryan, who told the Associated Press that security throughout the entire arena was, in her opinion, unusually lax.

It was in this unintentionally permissive environment that a large man in a black leather coat, black hat and khaki pants was able to position himself for what seemed at the time to be a random act of senseless violence. The man, with what appeared to be a legitimate credential of some sort draped around his neck, was spotted first by Kathy Stuart, a skating coach. In an Associated Press story published the following day, Stuart said the man appeared to be videotaping Kerrigan's practice session. She also observed that he was "sweating a lot."

Frank Carroll told *Sports Illustrated* that the same man had approached him and, pointing in Kerrigan's direction, had asked, "Is that Nancy Kerrigan?"

Carroll said that it was, but also thought to himself, "This is strange."

"He was an odd man. He was jittery, sweating," Carroll said. "He had a camera and he was taking pictures very fast. I didn't see where he went or whether he was the man who did it, but the next thing I knew, Nancy was on the floor, screaming."

At 2:40 p.m. an announcement had come over the public address system signaling the end of the afternoon practice session. Kerrigan walked off the ice and headed for her dressing room. She passed through a blue curtain into a hallway leading to the locker room.

The hallway, carpeted in red, was supposed to be a private area, accessible only to athletes, coaches, security and administrative personnel. Reporters were not to be admitted. Clearly, though, security was something of an afterthought, for when Kerrigan reached the hallway, she was intercepted by a woman named Dana Scarton, a reporter for the *Pittsburgh Post-Gazette*. Scarton wanted to fire a few questions at Kerrigan, and the skater obliged.

As they spoke, the man in the black leather jacket appeared from behind. He ran at them, silently, assuredly, as if on a mission. Quickly he wedged himself between Scarton and Kerrigan and swung what appeared to be a black metal rod at Kerrigan's right knee. The blow struck with such force that witnesses would later say the crack could be heard outside the hallway, in the stands.

Kerrigan fell to the floor and screamed—three times. Those screams, like the blow to her leg—the leg (not coincidentally, as it turned out) that is most vital to a skater's performance [she pushes off on her right leg when she jumps, and she lands on her right leg] could be heard throughout the arena.

"I heard screaming when I was walking away from the ice," Scotvold said. "All I could think of was, 'Where's Nancy?' I thought she was OK because she was not on the ice. But sure enough, it was her." He added sarcastically, "Great security."

A video camera captured the aftermath of the assault, captured in vivid images the sad and sorry spectacle of America's once and future ice queen lying on the ground, moaning in pain and fear.

"It hurts so bad," Kerrigan said through her tears. "Please help me."

As the crowd around Kerrigan quickly grew, security guards took off in pursuit of her assailant. For a moment, when he reached a Plexiglas door, it looked as though he might be stopped before he had a chance to leave the building. He would be captured, arrested, locked up, and revealed as the loony he was.

But this was a big man, six feet tall, 225

pounds. A strong man. And he was clearly not out for publicity, not interested in seeing his face on the evening news. He had no intention of getting caught, and so, he lowered his head and crashed through the Plexiglas door. He tumbled out into the street and was instantly lost among the hundreds of people who were in the area for an international auto show being held next door. He then sprinted away, into the snow, presumably never to be seen again.

Two

Back inside, Nancy Kerrigan remained on the floor, weeping, wondering who could have done this to her. Why *would* anyone do this to her? Kerrigan's father, Dan, was at her side now. He gently picked up his daughter and cradled her in his arms, as if she were not a grown woman, but rather his little girl again.

"I'm so scared," she sobbed. "Why me? Why now?"

That was the question of the day, and of the days to follow. Predictably, and not illogically, public response was one of outrage. It was presumed at the time that the attack on Nancy Kerrigan was merely another example of the decline of decency in Western Civilization—a brutal act of violence perpetrated on a lovely, charming young lady for no particular reason; a disgusting incident that lent credence to the theory that our society—America's—is the most violent on the planet.

This brutal act also sparked interest and debate and moral outrage on another level, most notably from sociologists and psychologists who specialize in analyzing the peculiar and frequently uneasy alliance between celebrities and their fans. Over the years, tales of twisted fans obsessed with rock stars and movie actors and television personalities have been all too common. A fan attempts to kill President Ronald Reagan to express his own deep and unending love for Jodie Foster. A woman breaks into the home of David Letterman—several dozen times. These are pathetic and depressing stories. And sadly, inexplicably, they are not unusual.

Until quite recently, however, such actions had been limited to the world of entertainment—fantasy entertainment. But in the months prior to the attack on Kerrigan, fan violence in its most bizarre, lurid form had moved squarely into the world of athletics. That should not come as a great surprise, actually, since athletes have become stars of the first magnitude. They earn millions of dollars, spend most of their professional lives in the public eye, and are supported, nurtured and molded by some of the best and most efficient publicity machines in the world. It was, then, probably inevitable that they would provoke the same sort of fanaticism previously reserved for stars in other areas of the entertainment industry.

So it was that in the minutes, hours and days after the attack on Kerrigan, speculation pointed to the likelihood that the assailant was a deranged fan. Images of a similar attack on tennis star Monica Seles in April, 1993 came rushing back, usually paired on television reports with pictures of the Kerrigan assault. Seles was stabbed in the back by a German tennis fan who was obsessed with Steffi Graf. It was his deranged mission to hurt Seles, then the top-ranked female tennis player in the world, so badly that she would be unable to compete for a lengthy period of time. (Incredibly Seles's assailant had the temerity to mount a defense of his actions: "On no account did I want to kill Frau Seles," Parch said at his trial. "I just wanted to hurt her slightly so that Monica wouldn't be able to play for a couple of weeks.") In that way, Graf, the number two-ranked player, would assume the top spot.

His plan worked, too: In January Seles announced that she would not be competing in the Australian Open, as originally scheduled, and that her return to competitive tennis had been postponed indefinitely.

There had been other strange examples of demented fan behavior, including at least two within the skating community. In 1992, two-time Olympian Katarina Witt of Germany was harassed by a man who repeatedly sent her obscene and threatening items through the mail. He was eventually arrested, convicted and sentenced to 37 months in a psychiatric facility. He also was ordered never to come in contact with Witt again. And there was a strange case involving Tonya Harding, who pulled out of a competition in her hometown of Portland, Oregon, in November, 1993, after she said she received a death threat.

"It's just horrifying," Kerrigan's sister-in-law, Tammy Moscaritolo, told reporters during an interview at Boston's Logan Airport shortly after the attack. "Why would anyone want to hurt Nancy?"

Kerrigan's brother, Michael, claimed that Nancy had never been stalked or harassed by anyone. She had never experienced anything but a warm relationship with the fans who came to see her skate. Still, the world responded to the news of her attack with the gigantic presumption of copycat fan violence. Kerrigan's twisted, weeping face appeared on the cover of just about every newspaper and magazine in the country. Columnists devoted thousands of words to the supposedly intertwined subjects of fan violence and inadequate security.

Generally, there was agreement that the world

is a sick place and always has been a sick place and always will be a sick place—and this was just another terrible, distressing example of that sickness. For her part, Kerrigan tried to remain upbeat. "I'm not going to lose faith in all people or anything like that," she told ABC television. "It was one bad guy. I'm sure there are others and this kind of thing has happened before in other sports, but not everybody is like that.

"The people who were worried about me, wondering what happened, those are the people I want to tell that I'm OK. It's not the most important thing—skating—so if I can't [compete] I'll have to deal with it. It could have been a lot worse."

Kerrigan's sense of perspective was deemed admirable by all who heard her words. That measured perspective did not mean, however, that she had ruled out skating in the nationals.

After the assault, however, fear began to spread to other Olympic athletes. "We compete in crowded places," said track star Gail Devers, the 1992 Olympic gold medalist in the women's 100-yard dash. "There is a lot of trust we put in the fans that they aren't going to harm us. But you can't help but think about it after you see what happened to Nancy Kerrigan and Monica Seles."

Shortly after the assault, Kerrigan was examined by Dr. Steven Plomaritis, who determined that her leg had not been fractured, but "the discomfort could preclude her from participating at her capacity." Indeed, that is precisely what happened. On the morning after the attack, the swelling in Kerrigan's leg, caused by a severely bruised kneecap and quadriceps tendon, had not so much decreased as moved. It now resided in the anterior portion of her knee, which prevented her from bending the joint fully. Doctors injected the knee with a local anesthetic and removed some fluid.

Kerrigan's range of motion was severely limited and the joint could withstand only a fraction of the stress it would be subjected to during a four and a half-minute free skating program. She tried to hop on the leg; the pain made it nearly impossible. There was no choice: she would have to withdraw from the nationals.

"I cried and cried," Kerrigan later said. "I'm pretty upset and angry that someone would do this, but I'm trying to keep my spirits up. I want to prove all this work hasn't been a waste."

The USFSA championships went on without their defending champion. Kerrigan's absence far overshadowed the performance of Tonya Harding, who, like Kerrigan, seemed to have discovered a new passion for the sport. Harding, a powerfully built (5'1", 105 pounds) skater, appeared fitter and more determined than she had in years. Not since 1991, when she posted a stunning upset victory at the nationals, had Harding skated with such confidence and style.

Harding's victory, though, and the runner-up performance of Kwan, were lost amid the swirl of publicity surrounding the Kerrigan attack. Even from the private box of Detroit Red Wings owner Mike Ilitch, where she and her seven-year-old cousin, Alison Schultz, watched the finals of the women's competition at Joe Louis Arena, Nancy Kerrigan was the center of attention. She was The Story, overshadowing the magnificent performance of Harding, who now appeared to be on the comeback trail, and the stunning progression of the waif-like Kwan.

Nancy Kerrigan.

What would happen to her? Would she heal? Would she ever skate again? And if fate smiled on her sufficiently to allow a full recovery and a subsequent return to the ice, what would happen to her dream of Olympic gold? The nationals were supposed to serve as the U.S. Olympic Trials. If Kerrigan did not compete in the Trials, how could she possibly qualify for the Olympics? Well, only through a loophole, of course—and there *was* a loophole. USFSA officials turned to their rule book and quickly underlined rule 5.05, on page 193. The rule states that the International Committee of the

USFSA has the right to choose athletes who, for whatever reason, had not skated in the previous nationals.

As Carol Heiss Jenkins, a member of the committee and coach of Lisa Ervin and Tonia Kwiatkowski, two highly ranked U. S. skaters, told *Sports Illustrated,* "We're not so cutthroat as a sport that we don't recognize the right thing to do. Even if one of my skaters were bumped because of Nancy, I'd vote for it."

Fortunately, a similar sentiment was voiced by Frank Carroll, whose skater, Michelle Kwan, was ultimately displaced by Kerrigan. A team is allowed only two representatives at the Olympics, and in light of the extraordinary circumstances surrounding Kerrigan's inability to compete at the nationals, and the prognosis for a full recovery, Kwan was demoted to first alternate.

"It's a tragic thing," Carroll said. "It'd be more tragic if Nancy wasn't given the opportunity to go. There's no question in my mind that if she'd competed, she'd have finished in the top two." Kwan, for her part, accepted her demotion gracefully, agreeing with her coach that it was "the right thing to do."

Those closest to Kerrigan predicted that she would come back from the assault, both physically and emotionally, in short order.

"Nancy Kerrigan is not a victim; she's a survivor," Cindy Adams, Kerrigan's sports psychologist, told *Sports Illustrated* after watching the nationals with Kerrigan. "That's how we're going to look at this. She doesn't understand what's happened or why, but she's not going to let this get in the way of what she's set out to do. She's going to be a little cautious around people for a while, but we should all be a little cautious. Nancy's not a worrywart. She's not someone who dwells on things. She's a strong individual, and she is loved a lot—and that helps a great deal."

Added Mary Scotvold, who choreographs Nancy's routines and helps her husband, Evy, sharpen Kerrigan's skating skills: "Nancy might be fragile mentally when it comes to her skating, but she's a tough little girl off the ice. She's not as vulnerable as she might seem."

Few observers of the skating scene had ever applied the word vulnerable to Tonya Harding. Her awesome talent notwithstanding, Kerrigan's chief rival had long been viewed as an interloper in the glitzy world of women's figure skating. She was not, and never pretended to be, a charm school graduate. Rather, Harding was brash and gifted and terribly driven to succeed. Often she said the wrong thing. Occasionally she angered and even embarrassed skating's elite, simply by being herself.

It was assumed, though, that she and Kerrigan would represent the United States in the '94 Games. While they were anything but mirror images, the two young women were, indisputably, the two best figure skaters this country had to offer. And, truth to tell, their differences could make for a neat bit of drama in Lillehammer.

Certainly those differences would make for great television: the delicate, soft-spoken Nancy Kerrigan, with her tasteful, feminine outfits, her perfect makeup and perfect teeth, in one corner; in the other, Tonya Harding, the cigarette-smoking wise-ass who cares little for proper public relations and, at times, even less for proper training.

The truth is, neither woman sprang from a particularly genteel background. Kerrigan's father is a welder from Boston's south shore who worked extra jobs to help offset the enormous cost of his daughter's skating career. Hers is, in fact, a decidedly blue-collar background, but she adapted to the image of a glamorous, gracious figure skater with relative ease.

Tonya Harding is something else. Oh, *is* she something else! Her background is hardscrabble, her life marked by violence and poverty. Skating rescued her, maybe kept her alive. At the very least, it gave her something to live for. Harding is decidedly unapologetic about her rebellious attitude, which can be traced to a dreadfully unhappy, impoverished childhood. She is what she is, and if you don't like it, well, root for someone else.

The image she presented at the nationals in Detroit was just that: fiercely independent and focused. Perhaps she wasn't mean, skating competitor Elaine Zayak offered, but certainly she was "cold."

In the aftermath of the Kerrigan attack, and her own victory at the nationals, while most of the world expressed stunned sympathy, Harding reacted with this callous statement: "It won't be a true crown until I face Nancy, and that won't be until the Olympics. And let me tell you, I'm going to whip her butt." The sheer insensitivity of Harding's comments spoke volumes about her character and, in retrospect, proved revelatory of darker currents that would soon swirl around the incident.

Small wonder that rumors began to surface, rumors about the attack on Kerrigan, and how maybe it wasn't a random act of violence, but rather a "hit" arranged by Kerrigan's rival, Tonya Harding.

Tough Tonya.

Crazy Tonya.

Pool-hustling, drag-racing, cigarette-smoking, trash-talking Tonya.

Unpredictable, uncontrollable Tonya, the self-described "Charles Barkley of figure skating."

And then composite sketches were passed around and people started talking and cracking under pressure, and pretty soon it wasn't just rumors.

Within days after the attack Harding's entire entourage was under suspicion. Within a week they were being hauled into court.

First there was her bodyguard, a hulking, 320-pound buffoon with delusions of grandeur named Shawn Eric Eckardt. Then the alleged "hit man," a 22-year-old Rambo wannabe named Shane Minoaka Stant. Then Stant's cousin, the driver of the getaway car, 29-year-old Derrick Brian Smith. And, finally, Jeff Gillooly, 26, Harding's ex-husband, allegedly the brains behind the whole perverted operation—an operation born of greed and hatred and a lust for power, and filled with so many mistakes and double-crosses and so much ineptitude that it rapidly became the tabloid story of the year, if not the decade.

All four men were charged with criminal conspiracy to commit second-degree assault against Nancy Kerrigan. Until January 27th, Tonya Harding had been implicated, but not charged. Then, in an emotionally charged press conference, Harding told the world that although she did not have "prior knowledge" of the attack on Kerrigan, she *was* privy to facts about the case which she had not shared with either the police or the FBI. Her place on the U.S. Olympic team was, for the time being, secure, but she was alone. The world, it seemed, had turned against her, vilified her for something she insisted she did not do, linked her to a sick plot to maim her rival, even though Harding, until the afternoon of January 27th, claimed to have no knowledge of that plot.

In her mesmerizing press conference, Harding, ever resilient, asserted that despite her mistakes, her lawyers had assured her that her actions—or in this case lack of actions—did not constitute criminal behavior.

So, as always, Tonya Harding stood proudly, defiantly at the center of the storm.

Just as she'd always done.

Three

There is a perception of the figure skater. As a woman she is elegant, proper, the embodiment of a traditional, perhaps antiquated notion of femininity. She is delicate, soft, non-threatening. The model has, admittedly, evolved somewhat over the years—power and speed, and yes, even muscle definition, are now acceptable in the sport—but it has not changed all that much. Nancy Kerrigan, after all, is not so far removed from Peggy Fleming and Dorothy Hamill. There is an innate charm to the figure skater, an ability to be part actress, part runway model, part athlete, part beauty queen . . . all at the same time.

Or maybe there is nothing natural about it at all. Maybe the behavior is learned, like any other behavior. As a small girl, the figure skater learns how to lace up her skates. Then she learns how to smile for the crowd and, especially, for the judges. She learns how to execute a pirouette. Then she learns how to apply just the right amount of eye shadow. Maybe her teeth are fixed, maybe her nose is straightened.

It's all in the name of art and sport, right? And anyway, most of the little girls who enter the sport of figure skating come from families that can afford the cosmetic surgery and the lessons and the equipment. Most can afford the annual tab of $30,000 that it costs to groom and house and refine a world-class figure skater.

Most of them.

Tonya Harding was different. She does not conform to the stereotype of the figure skater today, and she did not conform to that stereotype when she was a little girl. There was, in her childhood, little pampering or privilege. There was a good deal of pain and suffering, interrupted on occasion by brief flashes of joy. To her, though, those flashes of joy were merely a tease, and she learned to ignore them after a while. Skating, almost from the time she could walk, was her release, her means of escape.

"Tonya's come a long way. She's been very successful in her skating," her coach, Diane Rawlinson, said in an interview aired on CBS's *60 Minutes* shortly after the attack on Kerrigan. The interview was taped in 1986 by a Yale University student named Sandra Lukow, a former skater, as part of a class project. Harding was only sixteen at the time, a high school dropout from a broken and dysfunctional family who dreamed of chucking the shackles of a trailer-park upbringing in exchange for fame and fortune as the best figure skater in the world.

"I think everyone would agree," Rawlinson added, "that if Tonya had not had her skating, she probably would be a runaway right now and be doing a lot of things that we would not like to think of her into."

On November 12, 1970, Tonya Harding became the fifth child born to LaVona Harding. She was raised, however, as an only child. One of her siblings had died as an infant; the others were nearly grown by the time Tonya poked her head into the world. LaVona worked as a waitress in and around Portland; her fifth husband, Al Harding, Tonya's father, was a truck driver and day laborer who toiled for as little as $5 an hour. Back problems frequently prevented him from toiling at all.

The family moved frequently when Harding was a child—so often that Tonya has, on more than one occasion, been quoted as saying "I never lived in one place long enough to remember my address." All her addresses were in the Portland area. The family moved from one apartment or trailer to the next, packing up whenever their landlord decided it was time to raise the rent. Money was always tight, and so sometimes the Hardings would bunk in with relatives. Once, for a year or so, they lived in a mobile home parked in the driveway behind Tonya's grandmother's house. Like an army brat, Tonya changed schools virtually every year, which meant that every year she had to make new friends. Most of the time, she just didn't bother. She preferred solitude.

Her relationship with her mother was strained from as far back as Tonya can remember, but she adored her father. In a 1992 profile that appeared in *Sports Illustrated,* Harding acknowledged that the best times of her youth were spent with her dad. Al Harding had difficulty paying the rent each month, but he never seemed to have any trouble showering his daughter with affection.

Al Harding loved the outdoors, and he tried to share that with Tonya. She was just three years old the first time Al took her on a deer hunting trip. He told her it was important to keep quiet, and so each time a twig cracked under his boot, Tonya would press a finger to her lips and say, "Shhhh."

The following year Al and LaVona dragged Tonya along on an elk hunting trip. Mother and father left their little girl in the family truck on the side of a hill while they went off in search of game.

"She was a pretty good trooper," Al Harding told *Sports Illustrated*'s E.M. Swift. "Most kids would scream and cry when they saw mom and dad go walking down the mountain."

Much of this is the stuff of legend—Harding has often been accused of embellishing the hardships of her youth—but much of it also is true. Al Harding bought his little girl her first rifle when she was five years old; he cut down the stock so she could handle it comfortably. They practiced behind the house, taking shots at empty cans and tree stumps, whatever was around. She received her first deer rifle before her 10th birthday, bagged her first buck at thirteen.

"I was a better shot than he was," Harding once said of her father, and if nothing else the statement was a reflection of the competitive fire that drives her to this day.

According to the *Sports Illustrated* profile, Al Harding also taught Tonya how to fish. He would take her to the Columbia River to cast for sturgeon. While he fished, Tonya would walk the shoreline, searching for the heavy, ten-ounce sinkers other fisherman had failed to retrieve. The sinkers cost more than a dollar brand new, and Al would give her 25 cents for each one she found.

Sometimes the sinkers would be wrapped around brush and weeds, still attached to lines. Al enjoyed telling the story of hearing Tonya scream one morning after she had disappeared from his view. He was frightened, of course; he feared the worst—that his daughter had fallen in the river. When he ran to her, though, he discovered tiny Tonya reeling in a 41-inch sturgeon. She had stumbled upon a sinker on a snag, and as she unraveled the mess, she found, to her great surprise, that the fish was still hooked.

"The kid even beat you fishing when she didn't have a pole," Al Harding said.

It's an amusing anecdote, to be sure, the notion of a seven-year-old trying to haul in a fish her equal in size and her superior in strength. It speaks volumes about Tonya's desire to win, to be the best, maybe even to gain approval. Clearly it was important for Tonya to measure up in the eyes of her father. They were, for a time, best friends, sharing laughter and tears as if they were brother and sister, not father and daughter.

Tonya even helped Al work on the family car, a hobby that seemed harmless enough at the time but which would, as she tried to break into the stuffy and elitist world of professional figure skating, contribute to her reputation as a girl who simply didn't fit in.

But Tonya didn't care. She enjoyed tinkering with cars. It made her feel smart, useful, unique. She helped her dad change the oil, adjust the valves. These were lessons that stay with her even now: How many figure skaters—how many people, period—know how to replace a transmission or rebuild an engine? How many can replace the brakes on their own cars?

Tonya Harding can. And does.

"I was happy with my dad," Harding told *Sports Illustrated*. "We did everything together. But I wasn't very happy as a child. I was lonely. I never went to Knott's Berry Farm or any place like that when I was young. Skating was the only thing I did that really gave me confidence."

Considering her background, it is astonishing that Harding ever found her way to a skating rink in the first place. Figure skaters are ballerinas, often born into privilege and steered in the right direction almost from the moment they draw their first breath. Quite often, mom was a skater, at least recreationally. Maybe dad was, too. At the very least they share a knowledge of and a love for the sport, and that affection is handed down to the next generation.

Such was not the case with Tonya Harding.

LaVona knew nothing of Axels and toe loops and Salchows. She worked hard for whatever money she had—and there wasn't much—and she had few outside interests. Al liked the outdoors; he liked the winter, but he never equated snow and ice with figure skating, not in his wildest dreams.

Neither did Tonya. She fell into the sport almost by chance. Once exposed, though, she was infatuated, and her naturally aggressive, competitive personality took over.

"Tonya eats, lives, breathes, sleeps because she wants skating," LaVona once said. "And if that can't be done, if someone tells her she can't do it, she'll do it. The better and better she'll do it. With Tonya, if there's no 'You can't do it' type of thing, then she just won't do it."

Tonya Harding was introduced to skating when she was just three-and-a-half years old. She was shopping with her parents one afternoon at the Lloyd Center, in downtown Portland, when she spotted a group of kids skating on an indoor rink. Immediately, she felt compelled to join in.

"My dad said OK and my mother said no," Harding told *Sports Illustrated.* "So I cried, and finally she agreed. The first thing I did was make a pile of shavings on the ice and start to eat them. My mother told me I had to skate like the others or we'd have to leave. So I skated."

For Christmas that year Tonya's parents gave

her a pair of second-hand skates, and within a few weeks she was enrolled in group lessons. Unlike most of the other children, Tonya displayed something unique: raw talent. She was a bundle of energy, skating and falling and picking herself up again and skating some more, charting frantic little circles around the rink. She had no clue as to what she was doing, no idea what she was supposed to be doing, but she tried her best.

Think about it, though. What is it that would make a child of three-and-a-half so determined? At that age children are supposed to be carefree, innocent. Nothing bothers them, nothing really upsets them. Nothing really inspires them, either. Not for long. This child was unusual, though. She had to be dragged off the ice after each visit, reassured that there would be other chances, other days to skate. She was too young to be hooked, but she was hooked nonetheless.

Four

Later on, there would be debate about the decaying of Tonya Harding's relationship with her mother and criticism of Tonya as ungrateful. There would be accusations that she is prone to fits of temper and selfishness; that she can be sweet and caring one moment, petty and vindictive the next. It has, in fact, been suggested that Tonya's anger toward her mother, and a subsequent cutting of family ties, was merely the first of many "betrayals" in the young skater's life.

Tonya and her supporters, however, would argue that LaVona was abusive and demanding and sometimes cruel, and that Tonya simply did what anyone would do in that situation: fight back.

Before their relationship frayed, though, there was a period of time when LaVona tried to play the role of skating mom, awkward as it was for her.

"She can't come up to their standards," La-

Vona would later say of her daughter in Sandra Lukow's videotape. "No matter how hard she tries. And, of course, that just—that really gets to me. No matter how we try, I mean, it's always wrong . . . which is perfectly normal. I can't do good enough in anything. I can't feed her right, I don't get her to bed right, I don't do anything right. This is fine. I could care less. I do the best I can and that's all anybody can do."

They are generally referred to as "skating families," and not without good reason. One does not become a world-class figure skater without considerable assistance and support—and, yes, love—from one's family. Someone has to pay the enormous bills, and there are other considerations. If the little boy or girl (and usually they are girls) has to be at the public rink before daybreak to work on compulsory figures, someone has to do the driving. Someone has to bring the hot chocolate. Someone has to help with the homework. Someone has to choose the costumes and drive the young skater to competitions.

It is a strange and narrow world, as far removed from the spotlight of the Olympic Games as Portland is from Beverly Hills. Kids try to cram in a couple hours of skating before school. Then they join their friends and try, for a little while anyway, to be regular kids. But they can't, because regular kids—15- and 16-year-old kids—typically play soccer or basketball or softball. They watch TV and hang out at the mall and buy CDs.

They don't go to bed at 7:30. They don't do their homework every night before dinner. They don't have house rules prohibiting phone calls after eight o'clock in the evening, the way young skaters do.

To say Tonya Harding did not fit neatly into this type of rigidly structured environment would be an understatement. In many skating families, dad works and mom stays home with the kids. Dad writes the checks, mom delivers them. In the Harding household dad was often unemployed and mom worked crazy hours, trying to pick up enough in tips to pay the electric bill. There was a lot of yelling, a lot of fighting, a lot of tension.

There was not a lot of pampering.

They made it work for a while, though. Harding's dogged determination and drive—and obvious natural athletic ability—caught the attention of one of the instructors in the group skating program, who suggested to LaVona that Tonya begin taking lessons from Diane Rawlinson (then known as Diane Schatz) in nearby Jantzen Beach. When the Hardings drove out to visit Rawlinson, her first inclination was to reject Tonya, who by this time was four years old. Nothing personal, she said. She just wasn't accustomed to coaching students as young as Harding was.

"At first I said 'definitely not,'" Rawlinson recalled. "Every day for a week they had Tonya in a very, very frilly frock at the rink and she was skating circles around me while I was working with other competitive skaters. And I noticed that she did have a lot of drive, and she seemed to be very coordinated for a four-year-old, and I decided that I'd like to give it a try."

Tonya had similar memories of their introduction.

"My mom told me to go out and pester her for a while," Tonya told *Sports Illustrated*. "So I skated around her in circles and drove her nuts until Diane agreed to a six-month trial."

Some trial. While their relationship has had its rough moments, and its interruptions, the partnership between Tonya Harding and Diane Rawlinson has lasted more than 16 years.

"I could never pay Diane back for everything she's done for me," Harding has been quoted as saying. "Without her I would not be where I am."

Al and LaVona recognized their daughter's talent and love for the sport, and so they did what they could, including driving around Portland in Al's truck, scooping up empty cans and bottles they could turn in for nickel deposits. They would use the money to pay Rawlinson whatever they could, usually $25 a week in the beginning. As Tonya became more proficient, though, the costs mounted, until they reached the point where it simply wasn't possible for the Hardings to pay Rawlinson what she was worth.

All parties, however, agreed that Harding's talent was such that it had to be nurtured. She was tiny, yes, but she was powerful and gifted, and it would be wrong to turn their backs on that gift. So when Al found himself out of work, Rawlinson would donate her coaching time; she waived virtually all of her fees and even bought Tonya new equipment.

"Diane was really good to her," Al Harding told *Sports Illustrated*. "It costs $400 to $500 for a new pair of skates. We never had that kind of money. Tonya had to do more with less coaching than any of the girls she skates against."

According to Rawlinson, she also had to do more with less in other areas. There were problems in the Harding household, problems that were visible to anyone who spent much time with the family. In addition to being impressed by Tonya's natural talent, Rawlinson was impressed by her ability to overcome emotional trauma. At the same time, she knew that Tonya's troubled relationship with her mother would eventually present a major obstacle to her dream of winning an Olympic medal and securing the fame and fortune that comes with such success. For example, according to interviews in Lukow's videotape, LaVona's outbursts and harsh treatment of her daughter began costing the family potential sponsorship money when Tonya was still in kindergarten.

Rawlinson told the story of a local attorney who was revolted by what he saw one day at the Jantzen Beach rink.

"Tonya was in the corner doing jumping jacks. She was five-and-a-half years old. He fell in love with her and he sponsored her for a year. And the reason they stopped sponsoring her was because they were very upset with her mother's actions at competition time. A few times they saw Tonya's mother in the bathroom beating her with a hairbrush . . . using bad language in the lobby in front of other people . . . and they just felt that it upset them to see the situation at hand."

Antje Spethmann, who took lessons with Harding, supported Rawlinson's accusations of abuse.

"It's impossible to forget Tonya," Spethmann told the Portland *Oregonian*. "Even then, everyone saw her promise. She was great, a natural. The only problem was that horrible mother of hers. [She was] abusive and negative. She talked

like a trucker and called Tonya things like
'scum,' 'bitch' and 'stupid.' This was to a little
girl.

"She didn't care that other kids and their
mothers were there and saw what she was doing," Spethmann added. "She'd yell at Tonya
to say that she was making all these sacrifices
and spending all this money so she could learn
to skate and Tonya better be grateful. She
wouldn't let Tonya come off the ice when she
had to go to the bathroom. And all the time
she'd be yelling that Tonya sucked. I'm telling
you, she was a mother from hell."

Another skating mother, Pat Hammill, whose
daughter skated with Tonya as a child, reported
that she'd seen LaVona slap a preteen Tonya
hard enough to knock her off a chair.

It was Rawlinson's hope that Harding could
survive, perhaps even thrive, in spite of her
home environment. In time, Rawlinson knew,
Harding would progress to the point where she
would qualify for national age-group competitions. Once at that level, she might become eli-
gible for support from the USFSA.

Obviously it was a calculated risk. Certainly
the possibility existed that Tonya, a tempera-
mental, driven child, might just decide one day
to give up skating altogether. But that possibility only made Rawlinson more committed.
When she imagined Tonya without skating, it

frightened and saddened her. Too, there was the idea that she might have in her stable one of the most gifted young women ever to lace on a pair of skates. If she saw dollar signs, well, fine. She also saw what every teacher dreams of seeing in a pupil: brilliance. It was obvious to anyone who knew anything about skating.

"This girl is a Larry Bird or Wayne Gretzky," Larry McBride, owner of the Valley Ice Arena in Beaverton, Oregon, told the Portland *Oregonian*. "She's the best there has ever been athletically. There is not another figure skater who has ever laced up skates who could hold her skates. She has more talent than God has ever given anybody." Former Olympic figure skater Fritzi Burger, a two-time silver medalist, adds, "The skaters I talk to, we all think she's a better skater than Kerrigan. She jumps so well, she's more fluid, she has more speed."

Harding is a powerful skater, blessed with tremendous leaping ability. As the story goes, she landed her first triple loop at the tender age of nine, after another skater bet her that she couldn't do it.

Most skating prodigies eventually find that fear is their worst enemy: fear of falling, fear of injury, fear of embarrassment. Tonya is an exception to the rule. If she was at times quiet and withdrawn off the ice; if she had problems at home that made her question herself and seek approval from others, she seemed to be extraordinarily brave and confident on the ice. What others perceived as frightening, she merely saw as challenging.

For example, when Tonya was 14 she began experimenting with the move that would one day become her trademark: the triple Axel. It was an impossible move, a three-and-a-half revolution jump that even the best women in the world dared not attempt in competition. Tonya Harding fooled around with it in practice, landing awkwardly and occasionally falling, and knowing all the time that she would one day execute the impossible in front of an audience, in front of judges. She would make history.

"Most girls needed to be talked into doing some of the hard things," Antje Spethmann told *The Oregonian.* "Not Tonya. She'd try anything. She was fearless. The falls never bothered her."

"According to top skaters from Katarina Witt to Tai Babilonia, Tonya might be the most talented female skater who ever lived," her former agent, Michael Rosenberg, once told *The San Francisco Examiner.* "But it's a talent that needs to be refined and harnessed."

Harnessed is a good word, implying as it does that Tonya is something of a free spirit. Her spirit, from the very beginning, matched her athletic ability. And not merely her spirit, but her self-discipline, too. How rare in a child or teenager—or even in an adult—is the ability and drive to make the most of one's God-given talents? Tonya had that, at least when she was younger.

"She has this burning desire inside," 52-year-old David Webber of Portland told *Sports Illustrated*. "Her mother told me she never had to wake Tonya up to go to practice. That was all Tonya's doing."

Like Rawlinson, and a few others along the way, Webber befriended and cared for Tonya. They met in 1985, when he was the manager of a fast-food restaurant in the Portland area. In 1992, E. M. Swift wrote in *Sports Illustrated* that Harding had developed such a liking for Webber that she came to think of his family as her own. David was "Dad" and David's wife, Ruth, was "Mom." The three Webber children—Brent, Mark and Stephanie—became her surrogate siblings.

"If I ever had a family, they're it," Harding said. "They basically adopted me into their family. You don't need papers to be adopted into a family."

"She sort of adopted us," Ruth Webber said. "And we don't mind at all that she calls us Mom and Dad. Not at all. I don't think Tonya got a lot of love as a child growing up."

Harding herself has never been especially fond of airing the details of her private life, but interviews with her and with observers close to the situation present a picture of a child who cared immensely for her father, but not so much for her mother. And as she grew into adolescence, the anger and hurt became something closer to rage.

"Tonya's family loves her dearly," Rawlinson told Sandra Lukow. "Her mother just doesn't really understand how to get the best out of Tonya. She tends to put her down . . . to get her to perform. Her father loves her and Tonya would do anything for her father."

Tonya still adored Al, the man who had taught her how to hunt and fish and tune up a car. Mom was a different story. By the mid-80s, theirs had become an acrimonious relationship. They fought bitterly and often and over just about anything. At the same time, the Harding household was falling apart. Al's back problems kept him out of work for months at a time and LaVona was trying to work extra hours as a waitress. Tonya's aggressive and stubborn personality only added to the volatile mix.

Skating remained her salvation. It was her release, spiritual and physical.

"Her skating has really been her foundation in life," Rawlinson told the Portland *Orego-*

nian. "It's the only thing that has remained constant."

Tonya developed asthma when she was eight, and the condition— compounded by stress—afflicts her to this day. Even as her domestic life crumbled, Tonya climbed through the amateur ranks, progressing steadily each year until, in 1984, she earned a chance to compete in the junior nationals. There, as a 13-year-old, she finished sixth. She followed that with a fifth the following year at the Olympic Festival and a second at Skate America in 1986.

To the public, which was just starting to become familiar with Harding, she was little more than another promising young figure skater; one with unique ability, yes, but not one with such an unusual background. Few people understood the pain of her life away from the ice. They hadn't a clue. And for a long time, Tonya had no real desire to share that pain with anyone.

She did, however, share it with Sandra Lukow, whose Yale University videotape was snatched from the closet in the weeks after the Kerrigan attack, when the feeding frenzy for information on Tonya Harding was at its peak. Harding was just 15 when the tape was made, and if at times she seemed precisely that age, at other moments during the piece she seemed much older. At still other moments, she seemed much younger. She seemed at once confused and self-assured. Mostly, though, she seemed sad.

"Well, I'm really different from my brothers and sisters because my brother, he used to steal things and he still does," Harding said at one point, in an effort to describe herself. "He's like my mom. He doesn't have a lot of money, and he goes out and gets drunk and then he gets in fights and stuff. And, I don't do that."

The brother was actually a half-brother. His name was Chris Davison, and he and Tonya were not exactly the best of friends. One of the more tumultuous incidents in Harding's life, in fact, involved Davison.

This was in 1986, the same year in which Harding was interviewed by Sandra Lukow. As she later described it to *Sports Illustrated,* Harding was home getting ready for her first date with the man who would become her husband, Jeff Gillooly. Davison, 26 at the time, stormed into the house. He was drunk. When he found out Al and LaVona weren't home, he walked up to Tonya and attempted to kiss her. According to Tonya, it was the second time she had been forced to rebuff his advances. The first time, she stopped him with a slap to the face. This time it would not be so easy.

She grabbed a curling iron, then threatened to burn him with it if he did not go away and leave her alone. Davison kept coming, and

Harding responded in the only way she could: she burned him on the neck. Frightened for her life, Tonya ran upstairs and locked herself in the bathroom. Davison tracked her down, demanded that she open the door immediately. She refused, and so he broke down the door and stumbled inside. Another struggle ensued and Tonya was eventually able to break free and get to a telephone. Quickly, she dialed 911. By this time, Davison was in the room, watching her, listening.

"He told me, 'If you say something's wrong, I'll kill you,' " Harding said. "So when the operator asked me if everything was OK, I said yes. But she must have known that something was wrong because she called right back and asked, 'Are you sure everything's OK there? It's not, is it?' I just said, 'Yup.' "

The operator was right, of course. Everything was not all right. When Tonya hung up the phone, Davison approached her again, threatened her again, and this time she hit him with a hockey stick. Then she ran down the stairs, out of the house and across the street to a friend's. There, she dialed 911 again. This time she did not lie. This time she told them what was wrong. She asked for help.

While she waited, Davison left in his car. After seeing him drive away, Tonya walked back across the street to her house. She went inside and locked every door and window.

Then she waited.

And waited.

How much time passed? It felt like hours. She couldn't understand why no one would help her. Maybe they didn't believe her. Was that it? Did they think she was lying?

A car pulled up. Tonya looked out the window. She couldn't believe her eyes. There, on the front lawn, was her half-brother. Davison stood and stared at her. He pointed and shook his fist, screamed at her.

"I'm gonna get you!"

Then she heard a knock at the door. No, not a knock, really. Something more. A pounding, like someone trying to break in. They hammered at the door, over and over. They were trying to break it down, she was sure of it. She was terrified. She couldn't think straight.

And then she listened. She listened carefully for a moment, long enough to understand what was being said, and finally she realized it wasn't Davison after all. Well, yes, it was, but he wasn't alone. He had an escort.

Tonya opened the door and there, in handcuffs, was her half-brother. On each arm was a uniformed officer.

They made sure that she was all right, then took Davison to jail to let him sleep it off.

"That night I tried to tell my mom and dad what happened," Harding said. "My dad didn't want to believe it, and my mother slapped me and told me to get in my room. To this day she doesn't believe me."

She isn't the only one. Over the years more than a few people have suggested that Tonya Harding suffers from an overactive imagination. One of those people is Tonya's stepfather, James Golden, who, in a story that appeared in *Newsweek*, said that Tonya frequently embellished—and sometimes just invented—some of the bizarre events that dot her résumé. In general, he did not have many kind words for his stepdaughter.

"She was very selfish," said Golden, who, at the time of the Kerrigan attack, was separated from LaVona and about to become her sixth ex-husband. "Very surly."

Publicly, Tonya's mother, LaVona, has had precious little to say about her daughter in recent years. Two years ago, however, in that same *Sports Illustrated* story (a largely sympathetic pre-Olympic portrait, incidentally, although Harding reportedly didn't view it that way), La-Vona responded to Tonya's accusations about her half-brother.

"He did have a problem with drinking," La-Vona said. "I wouldn't put it past Chris to try and get a kiss. Tonya has a vivid imagination. She tends to tell tall tales."

When told of her mother's defense of Davison, Tonya stated, simply and coldly, that Davison later said to her, "If I ever catch you alone, you won't be around anymore."

He never did catch her alone again. Three years later, in Portland, Davison was struck and killed by a hit-and-run driver. Harding declined to attend the funeral.

"I know it sounds terrible," she said. "My mom tried to make me, but I wouldn't."

Mother and daughter did not get along then, and they do not get along still. But the Davison incident did not represent the nadir of their rocky relationship. Rather, it was merely one more battle in a long and exhausting war.

Much of the videotape produced by Sandra Lukow was devoted to Tonya's relationship with her mother. There was considerable anger from both sides, but Tonya came across as the more resentful, and bruised, of the two.

"My relationship with my mom is really bad," she said. "She is not . . . I mean, she's a good mother, but she's not a good mother. She hits me and beats me. If something goes wrong with work, then she takes it out on me. And everything she does, she yells at me or takes it out on me."

During one particularly telling scene, Tonya

was in her hotel room in New York, calling home after finishing sixth in the senior nationals. She had not given a terrible performance, but neither was it one of her best. Tonya had fallen in the long program and thus lost any chance of a medal, but her ability and grit had made people take notice.

That was the message she attempted to convey to her mother over the phone, and though the video camera and microphone recorded only half of the conversation, it was clear that Tonya was not getting the response, the approval, that she had sought.

"Yes, collect call . . . Tonya . . ."
Pause.
"Hi Mom! How are you? Is Dad still there?"
Pause.
"OK. I don't know if it's going to be televised or not. I don't know, but I got sixth."
Pause.
"Yeah, yeah."
Pause.
"No, that's good, cause now I get my international."
Pause.
"Well, tell Dad that it might be televised, I don't know. If it does, it—"
Pause.
"I got half a credit for it, Mom!"

Pause.
"*Yup. OK. Will do. Bye.*"
Hang-up.
"*What . . . a . . . bitch!*"

In the room with Tonya at the time, observing what to her must have seemed a fairly typical episode of familial discord among the Hardings, was Diane Rawlinson.

"What happened?" Rawlinson asked Tonya.

And from that moment on, Harding seemed less like a woman on the brink of national or international athletic prominence than a scared and wounded little girl.

"Mom said that, um . . . she goes: 'So, I heard you missed your combination. You know, you didn't get any credit at all for that.' And I said, 'Mom!' And she goes, 'You did terrible, you know that!' She said, 'You sucked!' And I said, 'Mom, I got half a credit for it.' She goes, 'So, the rest of the program sucked also.' And I said, 'Mom, you didn't—' And she goes, 'Well, just so long as you tried.' And I said, 'I did.' "

At that point Harding stopped talking. She sat motionless on the bed, wringing her hands, staring off into space, as if in a trance. Suddenly, she snapped into focus.

"Do you have a telephone book here? I'm hungry."

Perhaps she was making it up, or at least amplifying the ugliness of the conversation. Perhaps not. Certainly it seemed unpleasant enough.

In general, 1986 was not a good year for Tonya Harding. It wasn't bad on the ice, but at home there was only chaos. LaVona and Al were having trouble. Their marriage was coming apart. It didn't help that he was out of work and LaVona was exhausted from trying to support the family, and she and Tonya were bickering constantly.

Eventually, the strain took its toll. Tonya, who by this time had already dropped out of high school (she would eventually earn an equivalency degree from a local community college) to devote the majority of her time to skating, arrived home one afternoon to a near-empty house.

It was quiet. Quieter than she could ever remember.

The furniture was gone.

Likewise, six cords of wood she and Al had split themselves. Gone. All gone.

And so was LaVona.

"I stayed with Dad," Tonya told *Sports Illustrated.* "Mom didn't want anything to do with me. I remember she told me I was the only reason my parents had stayed together. That didn't make me feel good at all."

Father and daughter did the best they could after that, but it was impossible for Tonya to support them both while adhering to the rigorous schedule of a world-class athlete. Less than a year later Al was offered a job, which might have been a godsend for Tonya, had the job not been in Boise, Idaho. Having no real alternative, Al accepted the job and moved out of town, leaving his little girl—no longer so little—on her own.

She wasn't able to make it on her own yet, though, and so she moved back in with her mother, who by this time was remarried. LaVona and James Golden shared their home with Tonya until she was 18. It was a difficult two years, filled with emotional trauma that left scars on all parties. Even now Tonya's stepfather has very few kind words for her, noting, as he did in *Newsweek*, that if Tonya had the charisma and charm of Nancy Kerrigan, to go along with her formidable talent, "She'd have been on top a long time ago—and stayed there."

There was some disagreement over the circumstances surrounding Tonya's departure from the Golden house. Put simply, Tonya insisted that she was forced out; the Goldens claimed otherwise.

"My mother and her husband basically kicked me out," Harding told *Sports Illustrated*. "If I was to live under their roof, I had to live under their rules. They wanted me to pay rent or move out. I couldn't handle it."

LaVona denied those allegations vehemently. She also said she was hardly the portrait of the "bitch" painted by Tonya. "When I wasn't home, I was working. I did try," LaVona said.

"She couldn't wait to turn 18 so she could be with Jeff. I warned her about him before she married him. Then I didn't say anything else."

This would be Jeff Gillooly, the man Tonya eventually married; the man she eventually divorced; the man with whom she was living when the Kerrigan attack occurred; and the man who has been at the center of the controversy surrounding Tonya Harding.

Five

By 1990 Tonya Harding had become Tonya Harding Gillooly. Jeff Gillooly, a conveyor belt operator with the Oregon Liquor Control Commission, was the dominant male force in her life. But he was not the only one exerting influence. Indeed, one of the great ironies about Tonya Harding is that, for all her supposed independence, she seems to depend greatly on the approval and assistance of others—if only for brief periods of time.

One of these people—perhaps the most important one—was Diane Rawlinson, the person most responsible for shaping Tonya Harding the skater. She coached and trained, trying to make Tonya into something more than an athletic machine.

Not that this was unusual in figure skating circles. Skaters and coaches share huge chunks of their lives, and it's not at all unusual for the relationship to take on a familial tone, replete with anger and jealousy and territoriality. It is, almost by necessity, a relationship that runs bone-deep and because of Tonya's difficult childhood, the bond between her and Rawlinson was deeper and more intense than most student-coach relationships. Like the Webbers, Diane and Denny Rawlinson became a second family to Tonya.

Together, they tried to give her the love she had been lacking.

They also tried to orchestrate her career.

"Denny and I largely have paid for everything she's done in the past few years," Rawlinson said in 1986. "[Choreographer] Vicky Mills has donated her time; we have a costume designer who has worked practically for nothing; Highlight Skate Company from San Francisco has given us a good deal on the skates, and the rink has donated a lot of free time. But it's still really, really expensive."

Diane was playing Pygmalion to Tonya's Eliza Doolittle. She would take the street urchin with the legs of steel and the heart of a champion and give her a velvet sheen. She would make her more presentable, help her fit neatly into the stuffy skating community. That was the idea.

"Our plans for Tonya basically start with revamping her from her head to her toe," Vicky Mills said in the same 1986 interview with Sandra Lukow. "Hair, makeup, nails, clothing—on and off the ice. The total new Tonya.

"I'm looking to make Tonya into a skater, a little bit like Dorothy Hamill, a little bit like Peggy Fleming, a little bit like Linda Frattiani. Put them all together and mix them up so then we have a special Tonya. Because you've taken the best from everybody that's been the best."

Try as they might, they never were able to pour Tonya into a mold. She remained fiercely individualistic, almost as if she got a charge out of being different from the other girls, with their perfect teeth and their perfect noses and their comfortable upbringings.

They dressed conservatively.

She chose daring, provocative outfits.

They skated to classical music.

She skated to ZZ Top.

Tonya tried to act as if she enjoyed her "Rebel on Skates" image, but in truth the ongoing turmoil in her personal life was spilling over into her athletic life. She was unable to focus. As a skater, Harding showed scant improvement in those middle years, finishing fifth in the senior nationals in both 1987 and 1988, an Olympic year. For the first time in her career, there was some doubt as to whether she would ever fulfill her immense promise.

At the senior nationals in Baltimore in 1989,

the first held after Debi Thomas and Caryn Kadavy had retired from amateur skating, Harding moved up to third place. Her performance was impressive, though not quite impressive enough. Only the top two finishers at the nationals qualified for the world championships in Paris, which meant Harding would have to settle for alternate status.

"I thought I could have won at the worlds that year," Tonya told *Sports Illustrated.*

Maybe she could have, but she hadn't earned the right to prove it. Her response to that disappointment was one of indignation. If she had once been the model of self-discipline, she was now becoming almost cavalier about her skating. She was alternately hostile and sweet (a description that still applies, according to many of her closest friends). And she was, for some reason, not nearly as driven as she once had been.

In the months that followed the 1989 nationals, Harding trained less and less. Predictably, her relationship with her coach and mentor began to sour. After 14 years, Rawlinson decided she had had enough. At the very least, she felt it was time for a break.

"The bottom line is, it wasn't working," Rawlinson told *Sports Illustrated.* "Tonya wasn't training and wasn't meeting the goals she had set for herself. So I delegated her to Dody."

Dody Teachman, a former pupil of Rawlinson's, had developed into a pretty fair coach in her own right. Teachman had worked with Harding previously, helping her with her compulsory figures and cardiovascular training. Now, though, she was solely responsible for making sure that Tonya did not squander her ability and for helping her compose the proper ending to what should have been a beautiful, moving fairy tale.

"Tonya and Diane are both pretty stubborn," Teachman said. "They didn't get along very well by the time I got involved. They had spent a lot of years together. The older Tonya got, the more she wanted to do things her own way. My philosophy was to remember what I was like at that age. I knew Tonya had a rough exterior, and I'd heard all these horror stories, but I also felt that inside there was this nice little girl trying to get out."

Their relationship was less rigid than Harding's and Rawlinson's. They were coach and athlete, but they were also friends.

"Dody was more like a big sister than a coach," Harding told *Sports Illustrated*. "All I wanted to do was be happy, and I wasn't happy skating for Diane. Nothing was ever good enough for her. She tried to control everything. Everything. Who I'd talk to. How I'd talk to them. How I wore my hair. She basically tried to be my mother."

Considering what has happened since, it's interesting to look at Rawlinson's take on that crack in their partnership. At the time, she was cautious, diplomatic, mature. Much more so than Harding, she left the door open for a reconciliation.

"My whole association with Tonya has been like being on an adventure," Rawlinson said. "I wanted to be a wonderful, positive role model for her, and I feel very proud of what I did for Tonya and Dody both."

The new coaching arrangement was supposed to be better, healthier for all parties involved, but the following year at the nationals proved to be an even greater source of disappointment.

In Salt Lake City, in 1990, Harding skated well in the compulsories and short program. Heading into the free skate portion of the competition—which represents 50 percent of the skater's final score—she was in second place. She was in perfect position, mentally and physically prepared to make the leap to the next level—the leap to stardom.

As it often had, though, fate threw Tonya Harding a curve. She had been feeling weak and ill throughout most of her stay in Salt Lake City, and on the day of the free skate program her illness, exacerbated by her asthma, kicked into high gear. On the morning of her performance she had a fever of 103 degrees. She was told by doctors to stay in bed, but she refused. Gallantly, she took the ice, hoping that spunk and talent would carry her to victory and pave the road to riches.

It didn't turn out that way. Harding made just three of the seven triples she had planned in her routine and wound up finishing 10th in the free skate. Overall, she was seventh, her worst finish ever at the nationals.

"She was so humiliated from skating poorly," Al Harding, who was there that night, told *Sports Illustrated*. "But she told me, 'At least I didn't quit.'"

If she had given up the sport then, if she had walked away for good, quietly, humbly, her departure would have sent no shockwaves through the skating world. Tonya Harding had few friends in her sport; she would not have been missed. She was too rough around the edges . . . too unusual. She frightened people, almost challenged them to dislike her.

"People like her because she's a great skater, not because she's Tonya," said David Webber, whose daughter was one of Harding's closest friends. "She has an air about her that puts people off, an air of, 'If you don't like it, tough luck, that's me.' That's a hard way to make friends. You and I give a little and bend a little to make friendships and to keep them. Tonya doesn't. She has no security."

One of the few people who made her feel secure—in the beginning anyway—was Jeff Gillooly. After dating for more than three years, they were married in March, 1990, shortly after Tonya's dismal performance at the nationals.

"I never liked you," Al Harding reportedly told Gillooly at the reception. "But welcome to the family."

LaVona was no big fan of Gillooly, either.

"I tried to talk them out of getting married," she told *Sports Illustrated*. "I knew Jeff had a violent streak. Once when Tonya was living with me and my new husband, he tried to break down the door because he thought she had gone out with another boy. It turned out it was her brother she'd been with."

From all those who knew Harding, it seemed, Gillooly was getting low marks. Another person who came away unimpressed was Dody Teachman.

"He was a controlling kind of guy," Teachman said in an interview with Knight-Ridder newspapers. "Most of the problems I had with Tonya started with Jeff. We didn't see eye to eye on a lot of things."

In fairness, it should be pointed out that Harding's marriage to Gillooly seemed to rekindle her interest in and dedication to figure skating; less than a year after their wedding, Tonya experienced what surely was the high point of her career, at the 1991 senior nationals at the Target Center in Minneapolis.

There, on a cold February night in the upper Midwest, Tonya Harding proved all of the doubters and disbelievers wrong. She put on a stunning performance, rich in athleticism and courage and sheer drama. For more than four minutes she held the audience spellbound, enthralled, as she landed one triple after another. In a particularly historic moment, she landed a triple Axel, the first time any American woman had successfully completed that maneuver. Only Japan's Midori Ito had matched Harding's feat.

Imagine how it must have felt to her that evening, with the crowd rising to its feet and cheering for nearly a minute afterward, roaring their approval and appreciation. They had accepted her. They loved her. And so did the judges, one of whom awarded a 6.0 for technical merit, the first perfect score any woman had received in that competition in nearly two decades.

She was a winner.

An artist.

Finally, she was a champion.

One month later, at the world championships, the dream continued. Harding finished an impressive second behind teammate Kristi Yamaguchi. All seemed to be well in her life: her marriage was sound and she had found a coach with whom she could forge a solid, caring working relationship, built on mutual respect. Most important of all, she appeared to be happy, the effects of the abuse of her early years having all but melted away.

She was healthy and contented and rocketing toward stardom.

She was 21 years old and not even at her physical peak.

Surely this was only the beginning.

"Tonya was ready to do this a while ago," Teachman told *Skating* magazine in 1991. "It just took some time to put it all together and have it all peak at the same time."

As usual, though, long-term happiness proved elusive for Tonya Harding. Beneath the surface tranquility, her marriage to Gillooly was already straining. They fought bitterly, violently, though few people knew it at the time.

Quicker to come to light were problems between Harding and Teachman. With no warning, just one month after her runner-up performance at the world championships, and two months after the nationals, Harding announced that she was severing ties with the coach who had made her a household name.

If it was shock value Harding sought, she succeeded. To fire her coach just weeks after the greatest accomplishment of her career—a coach she supposedly loved and respected? What was she thinking of? What was she trying to prove?

This was crazy, even by Tonya Harding's standards.

"I was real hurt," Teachman told *Sports Illustrated.* "We'd had a couple of rocky phone calls, and she told me she couldn't work with me right now."

That was only part of the explanation, and not even the strange part. Harding, a classic example of a gifted pupil in need of proper teaching, announced to the world that henceforth she would be coaching herself. Well, not entirely. She would periodically solicit advice from her former coach, Diane Rawlinson, but mostly she was on her own.

Assisting the self-coached star would be Jeff Gillooly, who knew virtually nothing about skating but who knew his way around a camcorder. He would tape Tonya's training sessions and provide a strong shoulder to lean on. Later they would review the tapes at home and make the necessary adjustments.

"We worked well together and everything," Harding told *Skating* magazine. "But for the past two years, I've been in charge. I made all my own decisions. When things started to change and I wasn't in charge, that's when I decided to work with myself.

"I have my family and everyone behind me, and I have my choreographer, and that's basically all I need."

Another piece had been added to the puzzle, another chapter in the story of an extremely complex, volatile young woman. Less than a year earlier, when she was at her lowest point, Harding had been grateful to have Teachman on her team. Now, at the top of her game, she no longer needed her coach. She no longer needed *any* coach.

"I wanted this (championship) so much. I think just wanting it and training my own way is what made the difference," Harding said. "I worked hard from Pacific Coast up until two weeks before nationals. Every day the long program twice a session, the short program once a session. Then in the last two weeks I slacked off a little, but I still worked. I did the program once through. People were telling me to skate more sessions, but I did it my way, and—Boom!—I'm national champion."

The real reason behind their split had less to do with independence than finances. According to a story in *Sports Illustrated*, the breakup stemmed from a dispute over the distribution of USFSA training funds; specifically, whether or not Harding had given Teachman permission to sign her name when submitting expense receipts.

Teachman said she had; Harding disagreed. So the student flunked the professor.

Whether there were glitches in Gillooly's taping methods, or whether Harding was simply lonely and lost, the experiment in self-coaching did not last long—seven weeks, to be precise. Tonya went back to Teachman, contrite and apologetic. Teachman welcomed her with open arms.

"I went back and said, 'Dody, I need you,' " Harding told *Sports Illustrated*. "It was miscommunication. I learned you have to talk things out."

So they were back together again, a happy team: Dody, Tonya and Jeff—for a little while, anyway. Within a month, it would be Jeff's turn to be fired.

On June 17, 1991, not long after her reconciliation with Teachman and only 15 months after she and Jeff Gillooly were married, Tonya Harding filed for divorce. To some, the announcement came as a shock. One month later, in the July issue of *Skating*, Harding fairly gushed about Gillooly. The interview, which had obviously taken place a few months earlier, quoted Harding professing her love for Gillooly. They had put off their honeymoon for a year, and a recent trip to Europe had, according to Tonya, solidified their bond.

"He gave me an anniversary ring," she said. "It's super nice."

What is shocking to some, though, is mundane to others. Sadly, those closest to Harding weren't the least bit surprised when she left Gillooly.

"We were never in a competition where they weren't in a fight the night before we left," Teachman told *Sports Illustrated*.

In that same story, Al Harding, who has since returned to Portland, blamed himself for his daughter's marital discord. "I feel like I deserted Tonya when I went to Boise," he said. "I don't think she'd have married Jeff if I hadn't gone."

Maybe, maybe not. If Tonya Harding has at times seemed dependent on the kindness and support of others; if she has at times seemed easily influenced by those who should hold no influence over her whatsoever; if she has at times seemed willing to join in lockstep with the parade, there have been other times when she has marched to her own private beat, utterly blind to consequences and public opinion and protocol.

There was the night in Minneapolis, for example—the night she won the nationals in 1991. That night, after the competition and *during* a formal gala hosted by one of figure skating's most influential and powerful promoters, Tonya slipped out a back door and went off in search of a good game of nine ball with a few friends.

That's right—America's reigning ice princess was looking for a pool hall.

Six

Shortly after her separation from Gillooly, Tonya Harding went public with the ugly details of their troubled union. Only two days after filing for divorce, she petitioned for, and received, a restraining order barring Gillooly from coming in contact with her. He could not come to their apartment. He could not visit any of the skating rinks where she trained.

The marriage, as far as Tonya was concerned, was over. She claimed that Gillooly had been physically and emotionally abusive, and that she feared for her safety.

"He wrenched my arm and wrist and he pulled my hair and shoved me," Harding told a judge. That same year, in another police report, Harding claimed that Gillooly threatened to "break your legs and end your career" during an argument over possession of the couple's power boat.

That was supposed to be the end of the chapter. The marriage had been a mistake, just as everyone had tried to tell her, and now she had to admit they were right. Fine. She would move on. She would survive, just as she always had. If nothing else, Tonya Harding was a survivor. And after all, she still had skating. As long as there was ice and music and a chance to perform, she would be all right.

"My skating is my life," Harding said in a 1994 interview with the *Seattle Post-Intelligencer.* "I go out there and it's an out for me. I love skating. I have always loved it."

The divorce was to be finalized in November. In the meantime, Tonya moved in with Stephanie Webber. For a while she acted like a typical young adult, out on her own for the first time in her life. No parents. No husband. No fighting.

By all accounts, Tonya seemed happy. She gave Stephanie pool lessons. She went drag racing at the Portland International Speedway, thereby supplying more ammunition to those who would peg her as figure skating's renegade. The drag racing didn't last long, mainly because Harding's insurance company expressed great disapproval of it as a hobby.

According to an anecdote included in the 1992 *Sports Illustrated* profile, she also tried her hand at roller-blading—competitive roller-blading. In a televised celebrity event in Orlando, Florida, against a field that included speed-skating Olympians Elizabeth Manley and Bonnie Blair, Harding finished second, even though she had roller-bladed only a handful of times prior to the competition.

"She got back and said, 'I wasn't going to let all those girls get in front of me,'" Teachman said. "She should be on the front line of a football team."

That statement pointed to the apparent inconsistencies in Harding's personality. She could be driven, fiercely competitive, but she could also be lazy and unprofessional. For example, less than a year after observing that her skater had the heart of a football player, Teachman would say to *The San Francisco Examiner*, "If Tonya were to practice as hard as the rest of the girls, nobody could beat her. She would be unsurpassable."

Her training was supposedly going well in late 1991, after her separation from Gillooly. In addition to on-ice workouts, Harding lifted weights (she can bench press 110 pounds) and ran. She was in the best shape of her life—prepared, she thought, for the intensity of Olympic competition. A first-place finish at Skate America only served to solidify her reputation as a leading contender for a gold medal the following winter in Albertville, France.

Moreover, her personal life was on the mend.

She invited a young man she had met in Vancouver, British Columbia to come to Portland for a few days. He met Tonya's parents. They liked him. Close friends observed that Harding seemed almost blissful after his visit.

Then, inexplicably, just a few days later, Harding announced that she was reconciling with Jeff Gillooly.

"I'm a complete person now," she explained. "I know it seemed like I was happy, but something was missing, and now I know what it was. Jeff and I love each other more than ever. We're going to get a counselor and work it out."

They tried. Harding even took Jeff's last name for a while, becoming Tonya Harding Gillooly in competition. On the ice and off, though, the next two years were filled with more pain than pleasure for Tonya; more failure than success.

According to Teachman, Harding virtually abandoned her training regimen after getting back together with Gillooly. She did not resume serious workouts until one month before the 1992 nationals, which would serve as the Olympic Trials. She was unprepared for the competition, and no amount of bravado could hide that fact. Twice she attempted her famed triple Axel, and twice she fell. Harding was fortunate to hold on to third place.

"Reconciling with her husband became the most important thing in her life," Michael Rosenberg told *The San Francisco Examiner.*

"I don't think anyone can argue with those priorities. She continued to stay in shape, relatively speaking. She didn't just sit at home and get fat and lazy. But she didn't train to the extent that she probably should have."

The pattern of undisciplined behavior continued through the Albertville Olympics. Harding reportedly trained without a coach until two weeks before the Games. She arrived in France just three days before the figure skating competition was scheduled to begin—barely enough time to recover fully from the jet lag associated with a nine-hour time difference.

"If she had had a couple more days, she would have had her legs under her a little better," Teachman said.

She also would have had a bit more time to familiarize herself with the ice surface and to become desensitized to the potentially paralyzing aura of importance that surrounds any Olympic event. But Tonya Harding was typically stubborn. She wanted to do things her own way. So what if she'd never competed in the Olympics before? Skating was skating. She'd be fine. As for the time difference? No problem. Tonya had been all over the world and had never once suffered from jet lag.

The day before her short program, however, the veneer of confidence was stripped away as Harding tumbled roughly to the ice during a practice session. It was her habit during such mishaps to rise quickly and go on skating. This time she broke out in tears, sobbing uncontrollably.

It was not an encouraging sign.

By contrast, Harding's U.S. teammates, Yamaguchi and Kerrigan, had been in the Olympic village for ten days. Their problem was one of restlessness—how to fill all the hours without obsessing on the competition that lay ahead. Yamaguchi's answer was a three-day training trip to Megeve, located some 35 miles from Albertville. Kerrigan's answer was to come down with a nasty case of the flu. While hardly as enjoyable as Yamaguchi's diversion, it also chewed up three days.

Yamaguchi and Kerrigan each skated beautifully in the short program—which would account for one-third of the competitors' total score—finishing one-two. Harding and Japan's Midori Ito, considered less elegant, but more athletic, than Kerrigan and Yamaguchi, fared less well. Ito, usually a courageous and daring skater, decided at the last moment to substitute a safe triple Lutz combination for her famous triple Axel combination. It should have been a simple maneuver for Ito, a former world champion. Kerrigan had executed it in the afternoon; so had Yamaguchi. For Ito, there would be no problem. Remarkably, though, Ito fell during the triple Lutz, a blunder so stunning that a wave of silence fell over the audience. Ito, the favorite, stood fourth after the short program.

Bad as Ito's performance was, it was better than Harding's. The worst fears of the U.S. skating community, which suspected that Harding was not ready for the event, were realized. Unlike Ito, Harding stubbornly attempted her triple Axel; like Ito, she fell. Crashed was more like it. She wound up sixth and left without speaking to reporters.

"She's a little down," Teachman said. "She wanted to land that jump as much to prove it to herself as she missed it at nationals. But she'll be fine tomorrow."

Teachman's assumption was wrong. Two nights later, in her long program, Harding attempted another triple Axel and fell again. Overall, she skated well enough to finish fourth, but it was undeniably a disappointing performance, especially in light of her ascent to the top of the heap one year earlier. Her teammates, Yamaguchi and Kerrigan, finished first and third, respectively. Ito skated brilliantly in her long program to win the silver.

Tonya went home empty-handed.

"I certainly hope she learned from the experience," said Dody Teachman. "It would be a shame to have that whole experience be a waste."

If it was an education, her response to the lesson was not so much one of humility and self-awareness as of anger. Tonya lashed out. Three days after bombing in Albertville, she showed up at Teachman's home. They talked briefly. Actually, Harding did most of the talking; Teachman listened. What she heard, for the second time in less than a year, was this:

"You're fired."

Fine, Teachman thought. Have it your way.

"She's taken enough of my time," Teachman told *The San Francisco Examiner.* "I love Tonya. There will always be a special place in my heart for her. But she has a lot of growing up to do."

The explanation given by Harding—concern that Teachman's pregnancy would restrict the time she could spend with Harding—was flimsy, considering that in recent months it had been Tonya who was reluctant to practice. The deal was done, though, and Harding soon returned to Diane Rawlinson.

"Tonya wants to be the best she can be and realizes she has not had her training program," Rawlinson told the Associated Press.

"It has to be a team effort. She knows I am

a tough coach and she feels she would like to do it. She feels she is not the best she can be."

At the 1992 world championships in March, Harding began the process of re-creating herself. In addition to rehiring Rawlinson, she ditched all her old Olympic programs and showed up with new ones, even though she'd have only a month to perfect them. Her moves were new, her music was new (ZZ Top was exchanged for Frank Sinatra). So was her name: for the first—and only—time in a major international competition, she skated as Tonya Harding Gillooly. To further impress upon the world that their marriage was rock-solid, Jeff (who had by now quit his job at the liquor authority to devote himself full-time to Tonya's career) accompanied his wife to Oakland; it was the first time he had ever joined her at a competition.

"A month is not a long time," Rawlinson said of the sweeping changes. "But Tonya is involved in a heavy training effort. Conditioning, running, sprints. She has made a commitment to work harder. She's had a really rough year, but she realizes she can do so much more."

Tonya agreed.

"I'm more focused," she said at the time. "I have a team working for me. I'm more artistic.

I'm real happy about everything that's going on."

Her joy was short-lived. The downward spiral that had begun at the nationals continued in Oakland. Harding skated conservatively in the short program, not even attempting a jump until the routine was nearly half over, and was fourth going into the final. There, her athleticism deserted her again.

Harding skated last that day, making her performance all the more dramatic. Several women ahead of her in the standings had skated poorly, leaving room for Harding to at least snatch a medal, if not complete victory. Her routine was a mess, though. A sad, unpolished mess. Harding landed only two triple jumps; she doubled out of four others. The combination that sealed her victory at the 1991 nationals, the triple Axel, failed her again. For the fifth time in 1992, she attempted the move, and for the fifth time she missed.

When the scores were tabulated, Tonya Harding was in sixth place. Afterward, in an attempt to show that she could now handle disappointment, Harding tried to put a positive spin on the event.

"I'm a little bit disappointed, but I'm thrilled with the marks I got for style," she said.

Harding's coach, who knew what Tonya was

capable of doing, who had watched her as a child, was not so gracious.

"She tried too hard and she choked," Rawlinson said. "It's been a rough year for her. There's been a lot of changes and I think she's learned from them."

Meanwhile, the new Tonya was getting low marks off the ice as well as on. *Santa Rosa Press Democrat* columnist Michael Silver bemoaned Harding's transformation, saying, among other things, that while Harding appeared to be at peace during a preevent press conference, she also seemed "numbingly subdued, like the lobotomized Jack Nicholson in *One Flew Over the Cuckoo's Nest*. . . . Harding's retreat from her customary boldness is disturbing. It's like seeing James Bond shed his gadgets and surrender, or watching Pete Rose slide into home feet-first."

In other words, it was unnatural, and that bothered people. Here was another dose of irony. Tonya Harding, who had so often angered people simply by being herself, had decided to join the ranks of the conservative. She had decided to be exactly what they said she was supposed to be: sweet, demure, artistic. After all these years, she was trying to squeeze herself into the mold.

And now they were telling her the mold didn't fit.

She had no luck.

Fortunately, she also had no real desire to make the mold fit. The attempted transformation had been half-hearted at best, and it didn't last. It was fake, just like the image of domestic tranquility she and Jeff Gillooly tried to present to the public. He was supposed to be Tonya's emotional and spiritual anchor, but he was turning out to be something else entirely.

The rancor in their relationship continued unabated, though it was largely hidden from the public. From 1992 to 1994, their names appeared regularly in Portland police files, usually with Tonya listed as the victim, Gillooly as the suspect. One of their nastier arguments escalated into violence in March, 1993, when, according to Harding's version of the story (as chronicled by the Portland *Oregonian*), Gillooly grabbed her by the hair and slammed her face into the bathroom floor several times. She tried to run away, but Gillooly pursued her in his pickup truck.

A friend found Tonya in the middle of the night and brought her home. She was frightened. Clumps of hair had been pulled out. Her fingers were swollen—the result, she said, of having been slammed in a car door by Gillooly. She promised to leave him. Then. That very night.

Tonya Harding clenches her fists in triumph after completing her gold medal-winning program at the January, 1994 U.S. Figure Skating Championships in Detroit. (*AFP Photos*)

Tonya accepts her prize at the 1994 U.S. Nationals. (*AP/Wide World Photos, Inc.*)

At the 1993 U.S. National Championship (*from left to right*):
Lisa Ervin (second place); Tonya Harding (fourth place); Nancy
Kerrigan (first place); and Tonya Kwiatkowski (third place).
(©*1993 by Paul Harvath*)

Tonya triumphant as she becomes the only woman skater in America to complete a triple Axel jump at the 1991 U.S. National Ladies Championship. (*AP/Wide World Photos, Inc.*)

Tonya holding her first place trophy at the 1991 National Ladies Championship. (©1991 by Paul Harvath)

Tonya wins the 1991 Reader's Choice Award from U.S. Figure Skating Association's Skating Magazine. (©1991 by Paul Harvath)

At Sun Valley Rink in Idaho, Tonya appeared in a skating extravaganza headlined by superstar Brian Boitano and reportedly "stole the show." (©1991 by Shirley McLaughlin)

In the 1988 U.S. Nationals, Tonya's strong, vibrant style placed her fifth. (©1988 by Paul Harvath)

Tonya competed in the Senior Ladies Nationals for the first time in 1986 and placed a respectable sixth. (©*1986 by Paul Harvath*)

Her coach Diane Rawlinson chats with Tonya during her regular practice time. (*AP/Wide World Photos, Inc.*)

The small Beaver Creek, Oregon home Tonya shared with her ex-husband Jeff Gillooly until his arrest. (*AP/Wide World Photos, Inc.*)

LaVona Golden, Tonya's mother.
(*AP/Wide World Photos, Inc.*)

Al Harding, Tonya's father. (*AP/Wide World Photos, Inc.*)

Tonya's 1990 wedding to Jeff Gillooly. (*SABA*)

Sun Valley, Idaho, 1991. Tonya relaxes between performances at a skating extravaganza. (*SABA*)

Tonya escorted by her former bodyguard, Shawn Eckardt at the Portland airport on January 11, 1994. (*Brent Wojahn/The Oregonian/SYGMA Photos*)

Jeff Gillooly, 26, was married to Tonya for one year before she filed for divorce, claiming he abused her. (*AP/Wide World Photos, Inc.*)

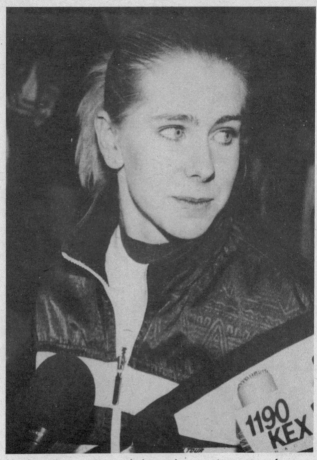

Her face shows concern during an impromptu news conference after a practice session on January 20: (*AP/Wide World Photos, Inc.*)

Tonya maintains her innocence after a grueling ten-hour interview with the FBI. (*AP/Wide World Photos, Inc.*)

Left: Shawn Eckardt, 26, Tonya's former bodyguard. (*AP/Wide World Photos, Inc.*) Right: Derrick Smith, 29, friend of Eckardt, arrested in connection with the attack on Nancy Kerrigan. (*AP/Wide World Photos, Inc.*)

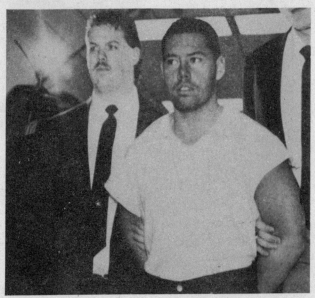

Shane Stant, 22, going to his arraignment in connection with the Kerrigan attack. (*AP/Wide World Photos, Inc.*)

Sarah Bergman, 20, a student at Pioneer Pacific College, a small vocational school outside Portland, escorted by Gary Crowe, private investigator and teacher of legal ethics at the college. Bergman is reported to have heard Eckardt implicate Jeff Gillooly in the attack. (*Bob Ellis/The Oregonian/SYGMA Photos*)

Eugene Saunders, 24, born-again Christian pastor, told Gary Crowe and investigators about a tape of voices that sounded like Eckardt and Gillooly planning an attack against a woman. (*The Oregonian/ SYGMA Photos*)

Despite all the scandal, Tonya remains as confident and feisty as ever. (*Reuters/Bettman News Photos*)

Not long after, Gillooly presented his side of the story to the police.

He said he would never hurt his wife, the report stated.

He did not hit her or pound her head into the floor.

It was Gillooly's contention that he only wanted to calm Tonya down. He followed her in his truck because he, too, feared for her safety. He wanted her to come home.

Harding was again granted a restraining order barring Gillooly from coming near her. She claimed, however, that he repeatedly violated that order. He continued to follow her in his truck, to threaten her, and she continued to call police for help.

"It has been an abusive relationship for the past two years and he has assaulted me physically with his open hand and fist," Harding wrote in a July 1993 affidavit. "Also he has put me down to the floor on several occasions. He is not in the right frame of mind, and he follows me and he has broke into my house and into my truck and I am afraid for my safety."

Harding claimed Gillooly stole a leather jacket from her house. She also said she received secondhand death threats. Gillooly denied all the charges.

According to one report that surfaced in

late January, though, Gillooly wasn't the only one supposedly threatening bodily harm. The Portland *Oregonian* reported that when Harding's truck was stolen in the summer of 1993, she suspected her husband. Harding was so angry that she approached two men with whom she worked out at a local gym and asked them if they might be interested in helping her "take care" of Gillooly. The men weren't sure what Harding meant. She had talked to them before about serving as bodyguards to protect her from her husband, but now, as they understood it, she was contracting a hit.

The two unnamed men, according to *The Oregonian*, were shocked. They said Harding mentioned a figure of $100,000, implying that she thought it could be done for less than that. A few days later, she returned and altered her request: Rather than having Gillooly killed, she now merely wanted him injured. The man interviewed for the story (though he was not quoted directly) said he was appalled; shortly thereafter, he said he stopped working out with Harding.

Neither Harding nor Gillooly would comment on the allegations. And, in fact, there is no police report to support the story, no separate allegations. There is no proof that the conversation took place, or that Harding was serious even if it did take place.

In August of 1993, a divorce was granted, but that was not to be the end of their relationship. Although she had dated other men during their separation, Tonya clearly had never purged her system of her love for Jeff Gillooly.

"She couldn't stop talking about him," Tom Arant, with whom Harding had shared a brief, intense relationship, told *The Oregonian*. "If I don't like someone, I don't talk to him. But she had to talk with him at least three or four times a week."

Arant said Harding seemed distracted much of the time. She repeatedly expressed her contempt for Gillooly and dealt with stress by smoking a lot—an interesting observation in light of the fact that Harding has always denied having any sort of nicotine habit.

In time, she went back to Gillooly, just as she had in the past, just as everyone suspected she would. But even their reconciliation was acrimonious.

It came in October of 1993. Harding left her apartment at three o'clock in the morning, following what neighbors described as a loud argument. Harding was putting her belongings in Gillooly's truck when neighbors heard a gunshot. Witnesses at the apartment said they saw a man pick a woman up off the ground and force her into the truck. They called the police, fearing the woman had been shot.

The truck was stopped. Inside, police found Harding and Gillooly, along with a shotgun and a handgun. Most reports stated simply that the two were taken into custody, but that no charges were filed. *The Oregonian,* however, reported a more detailed, and more alarming, version of the story.

> *A police officer handcuffed the world-class figure skater to the front of his patrol car and read her the Miranda rights. He talked with Gillooly in the back of his car, then with Harding. They said that the gun had gone off accidentally when Gillooly was carrying it, but their stories didn't match. The couple admitted that Harding fired the gun, but they didn't want that known, fearing the publicity. Gillooly admitted they had been fighting. About some woman he had been seeing. But he didn't press charges.*

No one knows why Harding was drawn to Gillooly, or why she was unable to break away. There are, however, theories.

"The question I always had when I was having problems with Tonya was how much of it was Tonya and how much was Jeff?" Michael Rosenberg—who cut his ties with Harding in the fall of 1993—told *The Oregonian.* "Because when Jeff was not around, everything seemed to go much smoother.

"I think she loves him and holds onto him and she hates him and is afraid of him."

The violence in Harding's adult life has not been restricted to altercations with Gillooly. There was a widely-publicized incident in Portland in 1992, for example, just a few days after she returned from Albertville, in which Harding got into a slapping match with a female motorist. The argument began when the other driver failed to turn right at a red light. Harding, in the car behind the other woman, and in a hurry, lost her temper. When Clackamas County sheriff's deputies arrived on the scene, they found Harding wielding a baseball bat.

"Ms. Harding told me the other car was trying to run her off the road," the deputy wrote. "And she grabbed the baseball bat to protect herself."

Harding later tried to soften the negative publicity that naturally accompanies such an incident, but she did a lousy job of it. First, she argued that it wasn't really a baseball bat, but a whiffle bat; second, she apologized through her agent, who said, "while it wasn't her fault, she regrets the incident and is sorry that it happened."

She did, however, pay for the cost of repairing the other driver's eyeglasses, which were broken during the argument.

Another strange incident occurred in November, 1993, when Harding received a death threat just an hour before she was scheduled to compete in the Northwest Pacific Championships at the Clackamas Town Center ice rink. An anonymous caller had phoned the rink and said that if Harding competed, she would be shot.

According to a story in *The Oregonian*, tournament officials and many of the skaters did not believe the threat was real. They felt Harding was trying to back out of the event because she didn't want to skate in a minor qualifier before the nationals.

"It was belittling for her to skate in this event," one organizer told *The Oregonian*. "She was a former national champion, had been to three championships and to the Olympics, and she was far and away the best skater in the group. Technically, she had to compete because she hadn't placed high enough in a previous event. They could have made an exception and let her go straight to the nationals, but because of her personality, they made her go by the rules and compete."

Because of her personality. Once again, it seemed that Tonya Harding was proving to be her own worst enemy.

Finally, the USFSA, after consulting with officials at the rink, agreed to give Harding a bye into the nationals. If the alleged death threat was indeed designed to spare Harding an unwanted performance, it had worked perfectly. The Northwest Pacific Championships went on without her.

Although it seems ludicrous that anyone would stage her own death threat simply to avoid the minor indignity of skating in a qualifier, it came as no great shock to those scheduled to compete against Harding.

"None of this surprised us," one skater told *The Oregonian*. "We were all wondering how she was going to get out of the competition. She thought it was below her to do it. She was not in competitive shape. A convenient thing happened. The thing is, she would have beat all of us."

Seven

The pictures lie. The image is false.

You've seen them, the medal winners posing together for the camera, arms draped around each other, each thrilled by the other's success. One big happy family.

You've seen them standing together, awaiting the judges' scores. They are in first and second place, and when the numbers come up, one will be champion, one will be runner-up. One will be an Olympic gold medalist, the other will be . . . quickly forgotten. Then it happens. The audience roars. The women turn to each other, embrace, smiling all the time, smiling so hard their makeup looks as though it might crack.

They must be polite.

They must be supportive.

They must hide their true feelings, because they are figure skaters and the world is watching and millions of dollars are on the line and they are expected to uphold the integrity of their sport, even if that integrity is an illusion.

Mostly, the image of camaraderie is a charade. A gimmick. Figure skating could hardly be more different from traditional team sports where group interdependence is crucial to victory. Figure skaters do not have especially warm feelings for one another. In truth, they barely know each other. They train hundreds, maybe thousands of miles apart. They see each other only a few times a year, at select competitions, and even then they have very little to say to each other, because they are, if not enemies, at least opponents, striving for the same sparkling, elusive prize.

They have sacrificed childhood and adolescence and even part of adulthood in pursuit of gold. They have chosen to exist in a strange world where success is dependent not only on grace and speed and athleticism and artistry, but on choosing just the right costume and hairstyle. A world like few others in sports, because in sports victory is supposed to be an objective thing: the team with the most points wins; the runner with the fastest time wins.

Skating operates differently. In skating the standards are completely subjective. It is as much theater as sport.

If you're a skater you accept the arbitrary nature of the game because you understand that it is precisely that air of drama that makes skating the glamour sport of the winter Olympics. Figure skaters are actresses, and the best actresses are paid handsomely.

How do you measure the value of a gold medal? What is it worth? Hundreds of thousands of dollars?

A million dollars?

Ten million?

Think about it. Sponsorship deals. Endorsements. Lucrative private contracts with ice shows and professional competitions.

Would you risk everything to get a piece of that? Would you hurt someone to get a piece of that? Would you close your eyes if someone close to you was willing to hurt someone to help you get a piece of that? Of course, it would have to be the perfect act of sabotage. You'd have to get away with it cleanly, because even being suspected of such a repugnant act would probably leave you branded as a leper by the advertising world.

But what if you could get away with it?

What if no one found out?

What if . . . ?

Between 1991 and 1994, Tonya Harding reportedly earned more than $200,000 from her figure skating. Minneapolis promoter Tom Collins told the Portland *Oregonian* he paid Harding $150,000 for appearances at his ice skating shows. Harding also received money through private donations, including $20,000 from New York Yankees owner George Steinbrenner, a big booster of the Olympic movement; $12,500 from the U.S. Olympic Committee; and $10,000 from the Tonya Harding Fan Club.

But figure skating is a costly endeavor, and the bills added up in the Harding household. Divorce records indicate that Harding and Gillooly fought bitterly last year over $9,000 sitting in a trust fund with the USFSA. In January, 1993, Credit Control Corporation sued Harding for an unpaid phone bill of $544.80.

When Harding and Gillooly applied for a Visa card at the Safeway Northwest Central Credit Union in November, 1991, Gillooly reported his monthly income from the Oregon Liquor Commission as $1,803.76. Harding, a "self-employed figure skater," listed her gross income as $1,800 a month. Two years later, in November of 1993, the credit union sued the couple in Multnomah County District Court to collect an unpaid Visa bill of $1,984. Also last year, Harding was evicted from her apartment after accumulating $1,095 in back rent.

Money was a problem for Tonya Harding. There is no doubt about that. Small wonder she said the wrong thing—again—when she returned triumphantly from the nationals in Jan-

uary, 1994. She was asked about being a champion, and about the Olympics, and even about
Nancy Kerrigan.

Harding's response:

"What I'm really thinking about are dollar
signs."

So . . . what if you *could* get away with it?
What if you thought you could get away with
it? Even for just a little while? What would you
do? Would you be tempted to do something
crazy? Something foolish?

A few years back Robert Goldman, a former
athlete and a scientist specializing in sports
medicine, asked a peculiar question of 198
world-class athletes:

"Would you take a pill, guaranteed to help
you achieve an Olympic gold medal, even if
you also knew that it would kill you in five
years?"

More than half of the athletes said they would.

Eight

By late January, 1994, the question of what Tonya Harding knew about the assault on Nancy Kerrigan, and when she knew it, remained unanswered. Authorities had, however, largely pieced together the puzzle. They had charted the actions of the four men arrested, uncovered a pathetically obvious paper and electronic trail, received confessions from Eckardt, Stant and Smith, and reportedly were prepared to bring charges against Harding.

The biggest flaw in their case was Eckardt himself. It was he who gave investigators the biggest share of the information needed to break the case. It was he who began pointing a finger at Gillooly and, later, at Harding. Much of what Eckardt told officials was corroborated after intense investigation of the facts. Nevertheless, Eckardt's credibility remained a central issue.

Described by virtually all who knew him as "a blowhard," Eckardt was a big man with big dreams—fantasies, really. He was a computer hacker who, at twenty-six, still lived with his parents and yet fancied himself a player in the daring fields of espionage and counter-terrorism. He threw out phrases like, "asset-protection strategies," made arcane references to attitudes toward penology in the 12th and 14th century, and described himself as "engaged worldwide in executive protection."

His résumé included such outrageous lies as "successfully tracked and targeted terrorist cells throughout the Middle East, Central America and Europe; coordinated and conducted successful hostage retrieval operations." According to the dates on the résumé, coupled with Eckardt's birth certificate, he would have accomplished these feats of derring-do when he was between 16 and 20 years of age.

Even when arrested for soliciting the services of a prostitute, Eckardt remained the fabulist, telling the police he was working undercover on a computer burglary case. (The 1987 case ended with Eckardt pleading guilty and paying a $125 fine.)

He was a high school and community college dropout who liked to pretend that he could arrange protection or mayhem; that he could move illegal goods, including drugs, if necessary. He was fascinated by guns and survivalism and wealth, and yet he ran his small business,

World Bodyguard Services, Inc., out of his parents' house.

He was also a boyhood chum of Jeff Gillooly.

"We're very much aware of the fact that his credibility is at issue," Eckardt's attorney, W. Mark McKnight, told the Portland *Oregonian* in late January, while awaiting word on whether a grand jury would indict his client, or any of the others. "Corroborating facts are going to be necessary or he'll be torn apart."

Multnomah County District Attorney Michael D. Schrunk acknowledged Eckardt's gift for spinning yarns, but he also said, "Everything Eckardt has told us so far has checked out."

So they knew what happened. Or they thought they knew what happened. At the very least, they had a story, a sick, twisted story involving a band of hopelessly amateur thugs—the Gang That Couldn't Kneecap—trying to pull off a caper that had virtually no chance of success.

Based on court records, statements, interviews, affidavits and reports from newspapers and magazines around the country (Eckardt granted extensive interviews to the Portland *Oregonian* and ABC's PrimeTime Live), the story unfolded as follows:

On or around December 16, 1993 (Eckardt said he wasn't sure of the precise date), Jeff Gillooly visited Eckardt at his parents' house.

They had known each other for years, and Eckardt had periodically provided "security" services for Gillooly, though those services usually amounted to no more than a few words of advice, and he was never paid by Gillooly. Sometimes, Gillooly would take Eck-ardt out to dinner to show his appreciation, but it never went beyond that.

This time it did.

Gillooly began talking about his ex-wife and Nancy Kerrigan, and about how much easier it would be for Tonya if Kerrigan were somehow unable to skate in the nationals. He asked Eckardt if, as a supposed expert in such matters, he might know anyone willing and able to hurt Kerrigan. Eckardt did not even know who Kerrigan was at the time, but Gillooly explained and Eckardt, impressed that Gillooly trusted him with this sort of request, said, Yeah, he could probably find someone.

According to Eckardt, Gillooly tried to lure him into the scheme with promises of fame and power and riches. The theory was that if someone attacked Kerrigan at the Olympic Trials, the entire sporting world—still scared out of its mind after the 1993 stabbing of Monica Seles—would respond with blind panic. Everyone would insist upon hiring a bodyguard . . . maybe 10 bodyguards. Eckardt, of course, would benefit the most. He would specialize in protecting skaters, and Harding would be his first client. (In truth, he had never before served as her bodyguard. The first time he would appear with Harding in public was upon her arrival in Portland after the nationals. Then, she said, she had hired a bodyguard out of fear for her safety in light of the attack on Kerrigan.)

It was a crazy plan, but it made sense to Eckardt. He, too, saw dollar signs. He would get rich. He would be famous, just as he'd always dreamed. He and Gillooly agreed to set the plot in motion. Eckardt said he would make a few phone calls, see what he could find out. And then he just sort of forgot about the whole thing.

One day, though, on approximately the 20th of December, Eckardt received a call from Derrick Smith, a one-time resident of Corbett, Oregon, who had recently moved to Phoenix. Like Gillooly, Smith, 29, had been a friend of Eckardt's for several years. The two shared an interest in paramilitary activities, and had even discussed the possibility of one day launching an "anti-terrorist" training academy. His home in Corbett, according to neighbors, was an exercise in paramilitary madness, with barbed-wire and bent-tree boobytraps surrounding the property.

Smith and Eckardt had gotten to know each

other when they were both taking classes at Mount Hood Community College in Gresham, Oregon. Neither graduated, and while Eckardt set up his own shop, Smith went to work for Developmental Systems, Inc., of Milwaukie, Oregon, a company that employed and trained mentally retarded adults. By most accounts, Smith was good at the work. He was quiet and patient, although some observers felt his behavior bordered on the anti-social.

"He did some wonderful things while he was here," Tom Cherry, the company's manager, said of Smith in an interview with the Portland *Oregonian*. "I've seen him do some wonderful things with people who would be most people's 'throwaway people.' I'm fond of him. I mean, there's a piece of him, if not all of him, that's a real good human being."

Smith and his wife, Suzanne, had often said they disliked the weather in Oregon, and most people who knew them assumed that was why they moved to Phoenix. But Smith had also talked about doing work for some people who planned to start a paramilitary camp in Arizona, and that was his actual reason for relocating. He had, on several occasions, told acquaintances that he would be doing work for a Swiss company, known as Blackstone, which supposedly specialized in counterterrorism.

Eckardt, a notorious talker, had also mentioned Blackstone to friends. In fact, he listed the company as a former employer on his résumé.

When Smith called that day he had no notion of the conversation between Gillooly and Eckardt; rather, he had a scheme of his own. He wanted to know whether Eckardt was interested in coming to Phoenix to help set up an anti-terrorist training camp. They chatted about that possibility for a while, and eventually the subject turned to other business. Did Eckardt have any irons in the fire? Smith wanted to know. Eckardt thought for a moment before revealing his chat with Gillooly.

He explained the rationale, how by disabling Kerrigan the path to Olympic gold would be much smoother for Tonya Harding. Gillooly thought that would improve his standing in his ex-wife's eyes, inasmuch as it would surely make her a millionaire. It also would allow Eckardt—and anyone who helped him—to become bodyguards to the stars. Moreover, Eckardt said, Gillooly had mentioned that the payoff would be substantial in other ways. For example, while he and Gillooly had settled on a figure of $6,500 to carry out the hit (an absurdly low figure for such dirty work), the assailants stood to gain considerably more by receiving up to ten percent of Harding's future endorsements.

It all sounded pretty good to Smith. He told Eckardt he could handle the job. He would enlist the services of his nephew, Shane Stant.

Stant, like Eckardt and Smith, was a survivalist and weapons enthusiast. He was also a rugged, sometimes hostile young man who carried 225 pounds on his six-foot frame and had scars on his face and head from beat- ings he had endured as a boy. He looked like a bodybuilder, which was precisely what he was.

"He bulked up during high school," Greg Schoenberg, youth pastor at Corbett Christian Church, told *The Oregonian*. "He seemed to me like a kid who just loved violence. He was always looking for a fight."

Sometimes he found one; sometimes he just found trouble. In 1991, for example, Stant and two friends were arrested for allegedly taking four cars from the parking lot of an auto dealership and going for a joyride. He spent 15 days in jail.

Stant was born in Corbett, spent several years as a child in California with his father, and then returned to Oregon when he was in sixth grade. He began lifting weights when he was a junior in high school and as his physique grew, so did his confidence.

"There were a lot of rumors about steroids. You just don't get that big that fast by lifting weights alone," Tony Lucky, a former classmate, told Knight-Ridder. "He was always talking about becoming a professional weightlifter and then becoming a bodyguard for wealthy people."

"He was the quintessential bully," observed another classmate. "He wasn't very nice. He had a hard time adapting to what other people wanted, what other people expected of him."

What Smith and Eckardt expected—what they wanted—was plain enough: They wanted Shane Stant to track Nancy Kerrigan down and hurt her. Just how badly she was to be hurt had not yet been determined.

A few days after Christmas, 1993, Derrick Smith and Shane Stant (who had lived with Derrick and Suzanne Smith in Corbett, and had moved with them to Phoenix to help Smith gain a foothold in the paramilitary business) arrived at the home of Shawn Eckardt's parents in a black Porsche 944. They wanted to set up a meeting with Gillooly. Eckardt made a call and they agreed to get together the next day. The meeting would be held at World Bodyguard Services, Inc., which might have been a problem, except that Eckardt's parents were not expected to be home.

They would have privacy.

They could arrange the maiming of a figure skater without anyone knowing about it.

Nine

It was Derrick Smith's idea to tape the meeting. He convinced Eckardt that Gillooly couldn't be completely trusted, and that the only way to ensure his loyalty was to record the entire plot. If there was evidence, they'd all have to keep silent. If one talked, they'd all be caught. This was insurance. That's what Smith said. What he was really thinking, Eckardt would later discover, was that this would also be a way to blackmail Gillooly; a way to guarantee that the bodyguard business would get off the ground, and the ten percent from Tonya's endorsements would arrive on time each month. Smith was no fool. He knew what he was doing.

Or so it seemed.

Gillooly was blind to the ways of the underworld, too. He walked into the meeting an hour late and immediately started talking openly about what he wanted done. Not specifically, but openly. He never noticed Eckardt's tape recorder on a desk, thinly disguised by a sheet of paper towel.

"We made the introductions and I sat down and Derrick told Jeff that he had come up from Phoenix to talk to him about his problem, and how he was the kind of guy who takes care of people's problems," Eckardt told *The Oregonian*, in an interview that closely matched his affidavit. "And then Jeff told them what he wanted done. He said he was looking for someone to make sure that Nancy Kerrigan didn't skate in the nationals."

The conversation turned gruesome at that point. Gillooly failed to make himself clear, failed to express precisely what he wanted done to Kerrigan, so it wasn't long before suggestions of murder were hanging in the air.

"It wasn't phrased exactly like that," Eckardt told ABC's PrimeTime Live. "Jeff used the term . . . he just said, 'Well, why doesn't somebody take her out?' And then I immediately came to the conclusion that it might have meant, you know, some sort of, you know . . . something that it possibly may or may not have been. I just sort of popped up real quick and said, 'No, we don't need to do that. There's other things you can do to disable somebody.' "

So they talked about staging a car accident, and they talked about breaking into Kerrigan's hotel room, tying her up and breaking her legs or cutting her Achilles tendon. Gillooly liked the idea of breaking a leg. He liked it a lot. He suggested they go for the right leg, which happened to be Kerrigan's strong leg—the leg she planted on when she jumped, and landed on when she came down. They ultimately decided to use a telescoping police baton to strike her on the knee. The baton was designed to cause pain and damage, but not break bones. It was the ideal tool for their plot.

That wasn't even the best of it. Before leaving the hotel room—or wherever it was the attack would actually take place—the assailant would drop a note. The note would be a warning, an alarm, declaring the attack on Kerrigan the act of a skater-hating psychotic. He was still on the loose, the note would say, and he promised to strike again.

Smith and Gillooly shook hands and agreed on $6,500 as a fair fee. They were giddy with excitement. All of them. It was a simple plan, a beautiful plan. They didn't even have to kill her, just hurt her enough to prevent her from skating. And the act would surely send ripples of fear through the skating community. It would be a financial windfall for all of them:

- The president of World Bodyguard Services, Inc. would have more business than he could handle.

- Jeff Gillooly would be the manager of an

Olympic gold medalist.

•Derrick Smith and Shane Stant would be able to start their own school for would-be Rambos in the desert.

Perfect.

"Smith liked the idea because it would possibly open up the door for more business," Eckardt said. "He wanted to take the proceeds from the protective service operations and open up this training facility. And he wanted me to run it for him."

Later they talked more about money, about how to get it and how to hide it. Gillooly asked Eckardt to compose a "threat-assessment" to be used as a plea to the USFSA for funds. If he could demonstrate that Harding's safety was at risk (he had the alleged death threat from November as evidence that it was), then the association probably would not deny the request. All along, however, Eckardt said the money was intended for Derrick Smith and Shane Stant; in effect, then, the U.S. Figure Skating Association would unwittingly help fund an assault on one of its own athletes.

The day ended with Gillooly handing Eckardt $2,000 in cash. Eckardt gave the money to Smith, who in turn drove Stant to the airport. Stant then took a flight to Boston, where Kerrigan was training, and where the hit was supposed to take place.

In Boston, Stant proved to be a lousy stalker. He tracked Kerrigan but never got close enough to carry out the plan. Meanwhile, from Phoenix, Smith repeatedly called Eckardt, who by now was acting as the official conduit between Gillooly and the hit men. Smith wanted more money. He said it had been promised and he wanted it delivered. He needed money to get around Boston, he said, and without it there was no way the assault could be effectively completed.

Gillooly was reluctant to wire any more money. He trusted neither Stant nor Smith, and as the days passed, he began to suspect that perhaps the two men had no intention of disabling Kerrigan. Perhaps they were simply trying to rob him a nickel at a time. Perhaps Stant wasn't even in Boston.

He wanted proof. He wanted receipts.

Smith, who was also growing agitated, wanted something else:

He wanted to punch Gillooly's lights out.

Cooler heads prevailed, though, and Gillooly eventually relented. He asked Eckardt to meet him at the Clackamas Town Center skating rink during one of Harding's midnight training sessions, on or about December 31. Eckardt, who had a history of back problems related to his weight, was in bad shape that night, so he had taken a prescription painkiller that left him feeling drunk.

At the rink Gillooly approached Eckardt and asked him to find a professional, someone who could really get the job done.

"And then he pulls out this $10,000 check from the United States Figure Skating Association," Eckardt told *The Oregonian*. "And I'm debating whether or not I should even bother with it. I should just let these guys break his legs."

Later, Eckardt said, Harding skated over to him at the edge of the rink and asked how he was feeling. When first arrested, Eckardt indicated that Harding knew nothing about the plot against Kerrigan, but later he changed his story in an affidavit to law enforcement authorities. He cited two or three incidents in which she spoke directly or indirectly about the plot. One of those incidents occurred at the midnight skating session.

"You know, you need to stop screwing around with this and get it done," Harding allegedly said to Eckardt.

Eckardt shrugged. "Why don't you call Stant yourself?"

"No, I want you to do it," she said, and then she skated away.

According to the affidavit, Harding also actively participated in the plot by making two phone calls to the Tony Kent Arena near Boston, where Kerrigan was working out. The purpose of the calls was to determine Kerrigan's practice schedule, thereby assisting Stant in his mission.

Telephone records indicate that someone did place calls from the Harding house to the Tony Kent Arena in Boston during the first week in January. Similarly, a representative of the arena said she did receive calls from a woman wanting to know about Kerrigan's schedule, though the woman did not identify herself.

Stant left Boston without completing his task. On Jan. 3, with money sent to him by Smith, Stant bought a Greyhound bus ticket from Boston to Detroit. Both he and Kerrigan arrived in town the next day. Smith phoned Eckardt to tell him that the assault would be carried out at the nationals. Eckardt told Gillooly, who did not take the news well. He suspected that Smith was stalling, trying to milk him for more money. That same day, however, Stant left a message on Gillooly's answering machine.

"Jeff, this is Shane. I'm in Detroit."

Gillooly smiled when he heard it. If not proof, at least he finally had some indication that Stant was actually trying to get the job done.

On Tuesday, January 4, Stant checked into a

$32-a-night room with a queen-sized waterbed at the Super 8 Motel near Detroit Metro Airport. His arrival was recorded by a camera in the motel lobby—the first of several mistakes made by Stant. He passed time in the room by renting and watching two videos: "Hollywood Fantasies" and "Girls of Beverly Hills." He then made several phone calls through the motel switchboard, thus adding to his own clearly-marked electronic trail. This man was not a master criminal; he was more like a member of The Gang That Couldn't Shoot Straight.

Gillooly withdrew $3,000 from the bank that day. He gave $750 to Eckardt, who wired the money to Smith in Arizona. Smith needed the cash so that he could travel to Detroit to drive the getaway car for Stant.

On Wednesday, January 5, Eckardt and Gillooly wired $1,300 to Smith and Stant in Detroit. They sensed that the new plan was going to work. Stant would have enough money to complete his assignment. He was to break or sneak into Kerrigan's hotel room, tie her up, gag her, injure her knee, and leave her to be discovered. On Wednesday evening, Stant phoned Gillooly from Detroit. They agreed that the hit would take place the following day.

Eckardt was awakened by a phone call around 10 a.m. PST on the morning of January 6. It was Gillooly. He was excited, yelling. He'd just heard on the news that someone had attacked Nancy Kerrigan; some maniac in a black jacket and black hat had just run at her in a hallway after practice and whacked her on the knee.

How about that?

A little while later the phone rang again. It was Smith. He told a similar story.

Eckardt was in a state of panic. After all the lying, all the stories, this one had come true, and now he didn't know how to deal with it. He went into the living room and turned on the TV. There he saw the pictures himself for the first time. He saw Nancy Kerrigan on the floor, holding her leg, her face contorted in pain. She was crying, screaming, asking the world—asking Shawn Eckardt—"Why me? Why me?"

Eckardt got up and turned off the TV.

Then he walked into the bathroom and vomited.

"I was very upset," Eckardt told *The Oregonian*. "I couldn't believe I had done this."

He had, though. He was in the thick of it. He was the middleman in a plot that would become one of the most intensely-covered news events of the year. And now there was no way out.

Ten

On Friday, January 7, Smith called Eckardt again. He wanted more money. Stant wanted more money, too. They needed $1,250 to finish the job, to get safely out of town and back to Arizona.

Eckardt phoned Gillooly, who immediately drove over to Eckardt's house. The two men then went to a Cub Foods store on Southeast 82nd Street in Clackamas and wired $1,300 to Smith. But that wasn't enough. Smith called Eckardt again on Sunday, demanding more money—another $4,600, which he felt would settle Gillooly's debt for services rendered. Eckardt called Gillooly again, and Gillooly said he would need time to come up with the money.

A few hours later, though, Gillooly boarded a plane for Detroit to be with his ex-wife when she skated for the national championship. He wanted to bring Eckardt with him; he wanted a "bodyguard" present so that it would appear as though he and Tonya were fearful of a copy-cat attack. But Gillooly didn't have enough money for another plane ticket, so Eckardt stayed behind with instructions to meet Gillooly and Harding at the airport when they made what was expected to be a triumphant return from the nationals. There, in front of an adoring crowd and hundreds of reporters, 320-pound Shawn Eckardt—owner of World Bodyguard Services, Inc.—would make his public debut.

By this time the outpouring of sympathy for Kerrigan was immense. The world cried for her, suffered for her. She received hundreds of letters, phone calls, telegrams, faxes, cards and flowers. One letter read: "We are so thankful you weren't harmed. We both know how difficult it can be to live in the public eye."

It was signed: Ronald and Nancy Reagan.

Meanwhile, as far as the public and the media were concerned, the assault looked like nothing more than the inexplicable act of a psychotic (though not a skater-hating psychotic—Stant forgot to leave a note). There was no reason to suspect otherwise. Police had recovered the telescoping baton outside Cobo Arena, and there was word that a fuzzy picture of the assailant could be seen in a videotape of the practice session.

That's all, though. That's all they had.

Supposedly.

Harding, skating to music from the film "Jurassic Park," performed beautifully Saturday night. She took first place, offered a word of sympathy for Kerrigan, and expressed fear that this could happen again, to somebody else. After all, the madman was still on the loose.

Harding and Gillooly returned to Portland on Monday, January 8, to a hero's welcome. Eckardt was there to greet them at the airport. He played his role perfectly, forcing his massive frame through the crowd to reach the diminutive skater, then cutting a path to the parking lane outside. He guided Harding to her father's truck; she drove off with Al Harding. Gillooly got into Eckardt's car; they sped off together.

Immediately Eckardt sensed that Gillooly was anxious about something.

"We have to talk," Gillooly said.

Eckardt knew what was coming. He was nervous.

"They asked me who Derrick was," Gillooly added. "I just told them I don't know what you're talking about."

The investigation had begun, and Eckardt knew now that the FBI was already onto them. Gillooly told him that they also had asked about Eckardt. They wanted a description. When Gillooly told them his friend weighed more than 300 pounds, the investigators were disappointed. At that time they still had not identified Stant as the assailant, and they were hoping that Eckardt's description might be a match.

There were many unanswered questions still, a lot of pieces to the puzzle floating around. Gillooly was confused. He didn't understand how it could be falling apart so quickly.

Where did the cops get Derrick Smith's name? How did they know?

Eckardt feigned ignorance. The truth was, he knew exactly what had happened. He knew that the whole outrageous and ugly scheme was about to come crashing down around them, because he was the agent of its demolition. Deliberately, stupidly—first out of some silly and pathetic need for attention, and later out of guilt—Eckardt had talked.

The expert in counter-terrorism and espionage, the man with a résumé that would make G. Gordon Liddy proud, had babbled like a child to anyone who would listen.

There was, for example, the meeting with Eugene Saunders, a 24-year-old minister from Gresham, Oregon. The two were classmates in a legal investigation course at Pioneer Pacific College in Wilsonville, Oregon, where they were studying to become paralegals. It was January 2, and the two men were working on a project together. But Eckardt didn't want to talk about the project. He didn't want to talk about school.

He wanted to talk about the meeting he'd had with Gillooly, Stant and Smith.

"He said, 'Here, I want you to hear something,'" Saunders told *The Oregonian*. "And he handed me a tape recorder to listen to. I said, 'Well, what's on it?' Because obviously it didn't have anything to do with our homework. And then he begins to explain to me that he recorded a meeting concerning a hit on Kerrigan."

Saunders could not understand most of what he heard—it was a poor recording—but Eckardt filled in the gaps.

"He began to explain that there was a meeting that took place, I believe at his home. He said Tonya Harding's husband was there. He said there was a discussion . . . concerning eliminating one of Tonya's competitors."

Saunders did not believe a word of it. He knew Shawn Eckardt. He knew about the lies and the bloated résumé, and he assumed this was just a particularly impressive example of Eckardt's overactive imagination. Saunders asked Eckardt to give it a rest. Eckardt refused. He continued to talk about the plot. Eckardt would later say he talked to Saunders in the hope that Saunders would turn him in; it was, he said, a form of confession. But Saunders later indicated that if it had been a confession, there was none of the remorse usually associated with such an act. Eckardt seemed excited about his story, almost proud.

The bragging continued over the next couple of days. Eckardt would corner Saunders and talk about the plot and the tape recording. Saunders by now was growing tired of the whole ridiculous affair, and so he threatened Eckardt.

"I gave him an ultimatum, basically," Saunders told *The Oregonian*. "I said, 'I can't keep it quiet. I will turn it in to the authorities.'"

Eckardt then told Saunders that the plan had been called off; there would be no assault. But a few nights later, at school, Eckardt approached Saunders and said, breathlessly, "Did you see the news?"

"No," Saunders said.

"It happened . . . Kerrigan."

Saunders was stunned. He didn't know what to think. He and Eckardt continued to talk over the course of the next two days, and Eckardt continued to back away from his story. He said he'd been lying, there never was a plot, it was just a hoax. Saunders asked for a copy of the tape, but Eckardt wouldn't give it to him.

The tape, incidentally, never did materialize; Eckardt said he burned it, out of fear. It should also be noted that Eckardt never once indicated to Saunders that Tonya Harding knew anything about the plot. On January 8, Saunders decided to talk with Gary Crowe, a Portland private investigator who also happened to be the instructor of Saunders's paralegal course. Crowe advised Saunders to take his story to the FBI.

Saunders was not the only person Eckardt talked to about the plot. Russell "Rusty" Reitz of Portland, also a classmate of Eckardt's, said Eckardt had engaged him in a bizarre conversation just two days before the attack on Kerrigan. For no particular reason, as far as Reitz could tell, Eckardt asked him if he would be willing to kill someone for money. Specifically, he asked Reitz if he would kill someone for $65,000.

"I thought he was kidding," Reitz told the Portland *Oregonian*. "I blew it off. I said no. He said, 'Would you break somebody's leg?' I said, 'Well, I don't know, Shawn, I'm not that way.' And he says, 'Well, I got a job in Detroit. I'm going to send a team there.' "

Reitz did not see Eckardt again until January 6, the day Kerrigan was attacked in Detroit. Eckardt was excited. He asked Reitz if he had seen the news.

"I said, 'Naw, I didn't see the news,' " Reitz said. "And he said, 'Well, Kerrigan got it,' or something like that. And I said, 'Who's Kerrigan?' And he said, 'It's the job I had in Detroit.' "

Like Saunders, Reitz was at first highly skeptical. He, too, knew all about Shawn Eckardt. He, too, had listened to the stories and the lies. Surely, he thought, this was just Shawn being Shawn, trying to be larger than life.

"I didn't even think he was really a bodyguard," Reitz said.

To his surprise, Reitz spotted Eckardt at Tonya Harding's side a few days later, on a TV news report. Eckardt was identified as the skater's bodyguard. The investigation was unfolding by this time, and Saunders's name had been tossed around in the media. Reitz heard one classmate's name, saw another on TV, and suddenly began to wonder if there was a nugget of truth in Eckardt's ridiculous story. He decided to call Saunders. They talked. They swapped information. Saunders suggested that Reitz call the FBI, and Reitz agreed.

The human trail was now nearly as long and plain as the paper and electronic trail, and it wasn't even complete.

Approximately one week before the attack on Kerrigan, Eckardt and another classmate, Sarah Bergman, got together for a cup of coffee at Shari's Restaurant in Gresham. They had been friends since August, when they enrolled together in Crowe's paralegal course. Eckardt had grown fond of Bergman. He phoned her virtually every day and often tried to impress her with his cloak-and-dagger stories. She liked him, found him amusing, but she also thought he was a bit odd.

On this particular day, Eckardt was in top form. He talked about Nancy Kerrigan and Tonya Harding and the figure skating championships. He talked about money and power. It was a rambling, unfocused story, and Bergman found herself tuning it out at times, but she understood the essence of it: Kerrigan was to be knocked out of the nationals. The reason, as she understood it, was to make Jeff Gillooly look like a hero in the eyes of his ex-wife. Bergman also came away with the feeling that Harding was aware of the plot, but she couldn't be sure. Eckardt wasn't clear.

What was clear was the payoff figure: $55,000.

"Shawn was one to tell stories," Bergman told *The Oregonian.* "You didn't know whether to believe him or not."

She didn't. Not at first. It never occurred to Bergman to phone the police.

On Saturday morning, five days before the attack on Kerrigan, Bergman stopped by Eckardt's house to use his computer. The phone rang while she was there. Eckardt answered and began talking. Bergman could hear only his side of the conversation, but she picked up certain words and phrases: "Detroit," "plane tickets."

Two days later she visited Eckardt again. This time he was upset. He was scared. He told her he was having trouble getting in touch with the two men from Arizona, the two men he'd paid $55,000 to assault Nancy Kerrigan. He accused the men of taking off with his money. He became enraged, at one point even punching a wall.

Bergman found the episode at once amusing and disturbing. For one thing, she couldn't imagine where Eckardt, who lived with his parents and drove a 1974 Mercury with missing hubcaps, would possibly get $55,000. She began to wonder if perhaps he was dealing drugs on the side. She remembered a previous visit with Eckardt, during which he had asked her if she knew anyone who might be interested in buying a pound of marijuana. To demonstrate his seriousness, he had pulled out a shoebox filled with what "looked like something he raked up from his lawn."

Another time he had asked Bergman if she knew anyone who wanted to buy a pound of crystal (methamphetamine). And more than once he'd displayed rolls of hundred dollar bills.

But on the day they met at Shari's Restaurant, Eckardt had told Bergman he had only $35 to his name. He was broke.

None of it made sense.

That was Shawn Eckardt, though. He was a riddle.

Two days later, when Bergman next ran into Eckardt, he seemed relieved. He smiled and laughed and told her everything was fine. Then, on January 6, she turned on her television and saw Nancy Kerrigan lying on the floor, screaming . . . and she wondered. She talked to a few friends, who advised her to call the FBI. An agent wanted to meet her in a public place, however, and Bergman balked. By this time she was frightened.

Another friend had told her he'd overheard Eckardt saying that he could have Bergman killed.

What could she do?

She could do exactly what Eugene Saunders did: talk to Gary Crowe, the man who taught her paralegal class at Pioneer Pacific College. He knew about such things. He could be trusted. Crowe met with Bergman shortly thereafter and immediately put her in touch with the proper authorities.

Another break—the first break, actually— came on January 7, the day after the assault, when a woman who refused to identify herself called Detroit police chief Benny Napolean to say she had heard about a tape recording made some weeks earlier. On the tape, a group of men, including Jeff Gillooly and Shawn Eckardt, talked about hurting Nancy Kerrigan. The woman had initially dismissed the plot as a joke, but when she heard about the assault at Cobo Arena, she thought someone should know what she knew.

Her story was added to the burgeoning pile of evidence in the attack on Nancy Kerrigan—and all of it was leaning toward Shawn Eric Eckardt.

Eleven

"I don't know where they got the name," Eckardt told Gillooly. "I didn't tell anybody."

They were still in the car. Gillooly was trying to figure out what had gone wrong; Eckardt was trying to stay calm.

They arrived at Al Harding's house. Tonya said goodbye to her father and drove off in the truck with Gillooly. Eckardt followed with their luggage. At his house in Beavercreek, Oregon, Gillooly still seemed distracted. He talked about the assault, and about the FBI. He was scared and angry.

"Jeff kept saying how we were all going to go to jail," Eckardt told *The Oregonian*. "And, you know, I'm just sitting there listening, and Tonya was getting upset. And then she started coming up with these excuses for the acts that she had done.

"She had made several phone calls back to (the arena in) Boston to try to find out how to get ahold of Kerrigan. And she said she was going to use the excuse that she had this poster with herself, Kristi Yamaguchi and Nancy Kerrigan on it. She had signed the poster, and Yamaguchi had signed the poster, but she needed Kerrigan's signature on it because she was going to send it to a fan."

Gillooly, too, was trying to think of excuses for his actions. But what? What could he say? The FBI knew about Smith. They knew a man named Derrick was in Detroit and that he was somehow linked to Harding and Gillooly and the attack on Kerrigan. Of course, Gillooly had no idea then that Eckardt had essentially already rolled over.

He struck upon a possible alibi.

"He wanted me to tell the FBI that I had surreptitiously sent Smith back on a sort of marketing expedition," Eckardt told *The Oregonian.* "To market to Claire Ferguson (of the USFSA) and some of the other figure skaters. And he told me to make sure I told the FBI that I did not tell Jeff because I didn't want to (anger him). 'OK,' he said. 'Let's get ahold of Smith and get our stories straight.' "

There was just one problem. Actually, there were a lot of problems, but the first was covering their tracks. They couldn't call Smith from Gillooly's house—they had to find a pay phone. And they had to get a disposable credit card, which, at one-thirty in the morning, would be difficult. After driving around for a while, they found a pay phone at the Jubitz Truck Stop on Marine Drive. They called Smith and discussed the alibi.

The following day, FBI agents asked Eugene Saunders to arrange a meeting with Eckardt. They asked him to wear a wire, which he did. Eckardt suspected something, though, and did not implicate himself. Gillooly, meanwhile, told an FBI agent in Detroit that Derrick Smith was working with Eckardt to set up a security service for ice skaters. He also publicly acknowledged that he was under investigation by authorities, but vehemently denied any involvement.

On the morning of January 12 Eckardt's mother woke him. Tonya Harding had called and asked him to get out to her house as quickly as possible; it was an emergency. When Eckardt arrived, Harding and Gillooly confronted him with a front-page story in *The Oregonian* detailing the first dirty news of the scandal: the possibility that Harding's entourage was involved in the attack.

"Jeff said, 'We've got to get some damage control. I'm great at damage control,' " Eckardt would later tell *The Oregonian*. Eckardt also said that Harding seemed relatively calm.

"She told me that she had completely convinced herself that she had done nothing wrong."

Eckardt wasn't nearly so confident. He was scared. He understood the situation completely. The police knew much more than Gillooly and Harding realized, and it was only a matter of time before they'd all be in jail. The game was up. Gillooly and Harding were hanging by their fingertips over an ever-widening chasm.

That night two FBI agents visited Eckardt at his house. They asked him a few gentle questions and he stuck to his story.

There was a pause in the conversation.

One of the agents asked Eckardt if he understood that it was a violation of the law to lie to a federal agent. Eckardt said that he did.

There was another pause.

"Then why don't you tell us what really happened?"

And that was it. Shawn Eric Eckardt bared his soul. He told them the whole sordid story. It was a real whopper, too, better than any he had shared with his friends over the years. This time, though, when he was through, no one laughed. No one rolled their eyes. This time they asked him to sign a statement, slapped a pair of handcuffs on him, and took him downtown.

On Thursday, January 13, Shawn Eckardt

and Derrick Smith were formally arrested in Portland and charged with conspiracy to commit second-degree assault, an offense punishable by a maximum sentence of ten years in prison and a $10,000 fine, though a term of one to three years seemed more likely.

On January 14, Shane Stant surrendered to FBI agents in Phoenix. Like Smith and Eckardt, he signed a confession.

On January 16, Nancy Kerrigan returned to the ice for the first time, saying that her knee was stiff, but overall she felt good and fully expected to compete in the Olympics.

That same day, the U.S. Olympic Committee, under pressure to make a decision on whether to remove Tonya Harding from the figure skating team, issued a statement. It did not specifically mention Harding, but did say the committee was determined to select a team that was "made up of America's finest young men and women who cherish the Olympic dream and who earn the right to represent the United States in a fashion highlighted by good sportsmanship, fair play, strong skills and a dedication to the rules of the game."

On January 17, Tonya Harding resumed training during a midnight session in Portland.

On January 18, an arrest warrant was issued for Jeff Gillooly. The same day, FBI agents questioned Harding for more than ten hours.

During a break in questioning, Dennis Rawlinson, the husband of Diane Rawlinson and also one of Harding's attorneys, issued a statement in which Harding announced, once again, that she was separating from Gillooly, although she still believed he was innocent.

On January 19, Jeff Gillooly was arrested and charged with conspiracy to commit second-degree assault.

On January 21, Tonya Harding skated in front of a crowd of more than 400 people—many wearing pink "We Believe in Tonya" buttons—at the Clackamas Town Center rink. There were placards that read: "Tonya Harding Is Back! Deal With It, America!" Her every move was met with applause. She continued to deny any knowledge of the attack on Nancy Kerrigan.

Over the course of the next week, news broke slowly. Gillooly spent nearly two full days meeting with investigators. Reports surfaced that he was considering cutting a deal in exchange for testimony against his ex-wife. Authorities also reportedly were close to issuing an arrest warrant for Tonya Harding.

Meanwhile, the United States Figure Skating Association and the U.S. Olympic Committee held numerous closed-door meetings in an attempt to devise a strategy for handling the delicate case. Harding had qualified for the team;

she had earned the right to go to Lillehammer. If they now tried to deny her that right, when she had not even been charged with a crime, let alone convicted, she would almost certainly take them to court. An ugly public battle would then become even uglier—and no one wanted that.

As the month of January drew to a close, the deadline for a Multnomah County grand jury report was twice pushed back, first to February 3, and then to February 18—six days after the start of the Winter Olympics in Lillehammer, Norway.

And three days before it would be too late to replace Tonya Harding on the United States Olympic Team.

Twelve

Tonya Harding skated for only 20 minutes on the morning of Thursday, January 27. She left the ice abruptly, seemingly shaken. Less than an hour later, accompanied by attorney Robert Weaver, she appeared at a hastily arranged news conference at a Portland athletic club.

Wearing blue-and-white sweats from the 1991 World Championships, and with her hair pulled back in a loose, girlish ponytail that made her appear much younger and more vulnerable than her 23 years, Harding stepped up to a microphone. At the time, no one knew why she had suddenly agreed to speak with reporters. It was known, however, that on the other side of town, Jeff Gillooly was undergoing his second consecutive day of intensive interrogation. Whether the two events were connected was anyone's guess.

There would be only a statement, Weaver

had said. Tonya would not, could not, answer any questions. Please understand.

Harding stood at the podium, her face almost blocked by the cluster of microphones in front of her. In her trembling hands she held a prepared statement. As she started to speak, her eyes welled with tears and her lips quivered. In the background, lights flashed, cameras clicked and whirred, capturing the drama—capturing, perhaps, the denouement of a story so strange it seemed torn from a supermarket tabloid.

"I would like to begin by saying how sorry I am about what happened to Nancy Kerrigan. I am embarrassed and ashamed to think that anyone close to me could be involved. I am disappointed not to have the opportunity to compete against Nancy at the nationals. I have a great deal of respect for Nancy. My victory at the nationals was unfulfilling without the challenge of skating against Nancy.

"I had no prior knowledge of the planned assault on Nancy Kerrigan. I am responsible, however, for failing to report things I learned about the assault when I returned home from the nationals. Many of you will be unable to forgive me for that. It will be difficult to forgive myself.

"When I returned home Monday, January

10th, 1994, I was exhausted but still focused on the national championships. Within the next few days I learned that some persons that were close to me may have been involved in the assault. My first reaction was one of disbelief, and the disbelief was followed by shock and fear. I have since reported this information to the authorities. Although my lawyers tell me that my failure to immediately report this information is not a crime, I know I have let you down, but I have also let myself down.

"But I still want to represent my country in Lillehammer, Norway, next month. Despite my mistakes and my rough edges, I have done nothing to violate the standards of excellence and sportsmanship that are expected in an Olympic athlete.

"Nancy Kerrigan and I can show the world two different types of figure skating. I look forward to being on the team with her. I have devoted my entire life to one objective: winning an Olympic gold medal for my country. This is my last chance. I ask only for your understanding and the opportunity to represent my country with the best figure skating performance of my life.

"Thank you."

When it was over there was only one question, from the one reporter who ignored Weaver's demand that there could be no questions. His voice came from the back of the room, loudly, clearly.

"WHAT ABOUT JEFF?"

There was no answer. Harding was already on her way out of the room.

After that it was a matter of deciphering the statement. Was it a plea of innocence or guilt? Or both? Clearly, she had asked for forgiveness. She had fairly begged for her spot on the U.S. Olympic team. She had said she wanted to win a gold medal for her country, but more than a few observers would suggest that she was digging for another sort of gold, and her country had nothing to do with it.

It was her lot in life now to endure the jokes and the criticism and the back-stabbing. If some people felt she was a victim, others felt she was a criminal. Worse, even. She was Amy Fisher on ice. And now she had to deal with it.

Shortly after the press conference in Portland, word came down that the United States Figure Skating Association had formed a five-person panel to examine the Harding case. The panel was scheduled to meet twice the following week before presenting its recommendation.

On Thursday afternoon, the U.S. Olympic Committee also expressed an opinion, and it did not seem to demonstrate much sympathy

for Tonya Harding. A statement released by
USOC executive director Harvey Schiller was
carefully worded.

And it was cold.

> *"The United States Olympic Committee is
> deeply concerned with statements made today by
> Tonya Harding relative to her stated knowledge
> of the attack on Nancy Kerrigan at the national
> championships.*
>
> *"We have been advised by the USFSA that
> it has appointed a hearing panel to investigate
> this and all other issues related to the attack on
> Nancy Kerrigan. In addition, the USFSA has
> indicated it will forward the names of 22 skat-
> ing athletes to us on Sunday (January 30) for
> the purpose of submission of the official entries
> for the Olympic Winter Games competition, and
> the list will include Tonya Harding's name.*
>
> *"As a matter of procedure we will submit
> those names to the Lillehammer Olympic organ-
> izing committee on Monday (January 31) under
> competition rules; however, the United States
> Olympic Committee is prepared under constitu-
> tional procedures to initiate any action deemed
> appropriate relative to any athlete entered in
> the Games. Changes in the skating rosters are
> permitted in each discipline well after the Mon-
> day entry date, and in the case of the ladies'
> competition, until February 21."*

Three thousand miles away, outside Boston, Nancy Kerrigan skated. Painlessly, confidently.

On the subject of Tonya Harding, she had no comment.

Epilogue

As this book goes to press, Tonya Harding has still not been charged with any crime; however, developments in the investigation have prompted a flood of reports indicating that her arrest may be imminent.

They include:

• On Friday, January 28, a Detroit television station reported that it had obtained phone records showing that ten phone calls to Shawn Eckardt's home were charged to Harding's personal telephone credit card on January 4 and again on January 6, the day Kerrigan was assaulted.

The station also reported another startling piece of news: An employee at the Detroit Westin Hotel, where most competitors stayed during the national championships, told investigators Harding had asked for Kerrigan's room number. Contrary to hotel policy, the employee gave Harding the information.

If true, this would turn out to be a vital piece

of information, because under Oregon law, the
testimony of co-conspirators is admissible in
criminal trials only when corroborated by other
evidence.

• On Saturday, January 29, *The New York Times*
reported that Jeff Gillooly, in exchange for information that could further implicate his ex-
wife, had reached an agreement with prosecutors. Under the terms of the plea bargain,
prosecutors would charge Gillooly with a single
count of racketeering and seek a maximum
sentence of two years in prison. The term
would be one year less than he might have faced
under the original conspiracy charge. Moreover,
a charge of racketeering can be wiped off a person's record after three years.

• That same day, Jeff Gillooly's brother told
the New York *Daily News* that Jeff had in fact
implicated Tonya Harding during the course
of his interrogation by the FBI—but only after
discovering that Harding had "double-crossed"
him.

John Gillooly said that his brother and Harding had agreed on an alibi. They had made a
pact. Jeff Gillooly broke that pact only when
FBI agents gave him a transcript of Harding's
ten-and-a-half hour deposition. According to
John Gillooly, Harding had told her ex-husband that she told investigators nothing, and
even when he was arrested the following day,

Jeff Gillooly refused to believe Harding had turned him in. It was only when confronted with details of Harding's interrogation that he decided to accept a plea bargain.

"His lawyer had the FBI come over with her 45-page deposition and let him read it," John Gillooly said. "(The FBI) told us she gave him up easily and coolly."

John Gillooly said his brother watched his ex-wife's press conference—during which she claimed to have had no advance knowledge of that attack on Nancy Kerrigan—while surrounded by investigators. According to John Gillooly, Jeff said, "The FBI were laughing at her."

"They're talking about crucifying her because she has the audacity to be skating in the Olympics in the face of all this," John Gillooly told *The Daily News*. "They're taking this as an insult because she won't have the good grace to bow out."

As of January 30, 1994, there has been no change of heart. Tonya Harding remains a member of the U.S. Olympic team.

• On January 31, NIKE chief executive officer Philip Knight began playing the role of white knight. He announced that his company would contribute $25,000 to help Harding defend herself in the event that the U.S. Olympic Committee tried to remove her from the team before she was found guilty of a crime.

•On February 1, Jeff Gillooly appeared before Multnomah County Circuit Court Judge David Londer and pleaded guilty to his role in the attack on Nancy Kerrigan. Gillooly, speaking quietly and somberly, struck a plea bargain in which he confessed to a single charge of racketeering in exchange for his testimony implicating his ex-wife Tonya Harding. Under the agreement, Gillooly will be sentenced—providing he abides by the conditions of the plea agreement—to 24 months in a federal prison and be fined $100,000 in exchange for testifying "truly and fully" in all investigations and trials involving the assault on Nancy Kerrigan. Formal sentencing was set for April 1, 1994.

Gillooly did not speak to reporters: however, his lawyer, Ron Hoevet, issued the following statement:

> *"Jeff Gillooly pled guilty today to violating the Oregon racketeering statute. In his plea, Jeff admitted to offenses which helped further the assault on Nancy Kerrigan. By truthfully telling all he knows regarding the assault and the cover-up to state and federal law enforcement officials and the Multnomah County grand jury, he has resolved the case against him in*

Oregon and in all other federal and state juris-dictions.

"Jeff is not here today. He has a continuing duty to cooperate with state and federal law en-forcement officials in the investigation and prosecution of others who were involved in this crime.

"It is unlikely that he will make any public statement before that duty is fulfilled. Most of Jeff's seventeen and one-half hour statement to the FBI last Wednesday and Thursday has been released today by the district attorney. It an-swers the questions you want to know. What did Tonya Harding know and when did she know it? What did she do to further the assault on Nancy Kerrigan and to cover it up?

"The key date is December 28, 1993. That morning, Jeff met with Shawn Eckardt, Derrick Smith and Shane Stant in Eckardt's home. Tonya knew that the purpose of this meeting was to discuss how they could prevent Nancy Kerrigan from competing for the U.S. Women's Figure Skating Championship. Tonya dropped Jeff off at the meeting and picked him up after it was over.

"Jeff took to that meeting approximately $3,000 in cash, the name of the rink where Nancy Ker-rigan practiced, and her photograph.

"Tonya had personally obtained the name of the Tony Kent Arena a day or two before the

*meeting. After the meeting, while driving to-
ward home, Tonya approved the plan that had
been discussed and gave the OK for the assault
on Nancy Kerrigan. The final decision was hers
to make.*

*"That same afternoon, Tonya called the Tony
Kent Arena from her home to determine Nancy
Kerrigan's practice schedule. Later that same
evening, Jeff and Tonya returned to Eckardt's
house. Jeff paid Eckardt $2,000 and Tonya pro-
vided additional information about Nancy Kerrigan, including a magazine article which
contained her full-page picture.*

*"When the assault had not taken place by
New Year's Eve, Tonya became upset. About
midnight on January 1, 1994, she confronted
Shawn Eckardt and Jeff at the Ice Chalet in
Clackamas Town Center. She complained that
no one seemed to be able 'to do this thing for
her' and demanded her $2,000 back from
Eckardt.*

*"After Tonya arrived in Detroit and learned
that Smith and Shane Stant had also traveled
there, she personally obtained the room number
of Nancy Kerrigan and her practice schedule,
she forwarded this information on to Jeff in Portland, who faxed it to Eckardt, who then relayed
it to Smith and Stant in Detroit.*

*"After the assault on Nancy Kerrigan on
January 6, 1994, the FBI received an anony-*

mous tip while Jeff and Tonya were in Detroit. The tip implicated Jeff, Tonya, Eckardt and Smith in the crime. When Jeff and Tonya returned to Portland the night of January 10, 1994, they were surveilled by the FBI and other law enforcement officers. The authorities watched as Jeff, Tonya and Eckardt met to create a cover story.

"They watched as Jeff, Tonya and Eckardt made telephone calls to Smith on Monday night and Tuesday morning from public telephones with a 'talk-and-toss' card to set the cover story straight. They watched as Jeff and Tonya drove by Eckardt's house again and again Tuesday night and early Wednesday morning in an attempt to monitor Eckardt's interview with the FBI.

"They watched as Jeff and Tonya drove to Elmer's Pancake House and reconnoitered the parking lot to see if the FBI were there. Before entering the restaurant to meet with Eckardt, who was wired, Jeff handed his wallet and watch to Tonya because both of them believed he was going to be arrested inside.

"Jeff and I have known each other less than three weeks. In those few days, however, we have traveled a long way together, from denial to acceptance. I know Jeff deeply regrets his involvement in this crime. He knows he and others have brought pain and fear to Nancy Kerrigan,

her family and her fans. By this plea and co-operation agreement, Jeff hopes to bring closure to his own involvement in these events.

"Finally, Jeff has a message for Tonya—he hopes that she will know what he has done and move quickly to resolve the charges that will surely be brought against her.

"And I would like to add something as well: Tonya is well-represented by Bob Weaver, my good friend and former trial partner at the U.S. attorney's office. She should listen to him. He can help her. Denial is no longer plausible. The truth about this bizarre crime has now been revealed."

Tonya Harding's response was swift and unrepentant. Through her attorneys, she issued the following statement:

"Jeff Gillooly's accusations appear to evidence a continued practice of abusive conduct intended to disrupt Tonya Harding's life and destroy her career.

"Tonya Harding denies Mr. Gillooly's accusations and all media speculation and rumors that suggest that she was involved in the Kerrigan assault.

"Tonya Harding is dedicating her full attention to preparation for the Olympics.

"On a separate note, we are proud of Phil

*Knight and NIKE, Inc., for their courageous
showing of support. We are extremely disappointed that the United States Olympic Committee, whose constitution mandates that it use
all lawful means 'to protect the right of an amateur athlete to participate . . . in the Olympic
Games' has not, as yet, made a similar showing
of support."*

As of February 1, 1994, Tonya Harding had
not been charged with any crime.

Appendix A

THIN ICE: A CHRONOLOGY

The following day-by-day account is based on information taken from affidavits, news reports, bank and phone company records, public statements by those involved.

December 16 or 17

Jeff Gillooly approaches Shawn Eckardt (according to Eckardt) to discuss a plan to assault Nancy Kerrigan.

December 27

According to bank records, Gillooly withdraws $3,000 from his account at a Portland bank.

December 27 or 28

According to Eckardt (who is unsure of the date):

●Gillooly, Shane Stant and Derrick Smith meet with Eckardt at his home to discuss their plot against Kerrigan;

●They agree that Gillooly will pay Stant and Smith $6,500 to commit an assault on Kerrigan;

●Gillooly tells Stant to hit Kerrigan in the right knee, since she lands on her right leg after jumps;

●Gillooly gives Eckardt $,2000, which Eckardt subsequently gives to Smith.

December 28

Phone company records show that calls are made from the Gillooly/Harding home to Kerrigan's home rink.

Shane Stant departs Portland for Boston.

December 29

Stant flies into Boston, stays at a hotel near the airport, then moves to Cape Cod, near Kerrigan's practice rink.

January 1

Stant calls Kerrigan's rink from his motel room.

January 2

Eckardt tells Eugene Saunders, a fellow student and born-again "minister," that he is part of a plot to harm Nancy Kerrigan.

Eckardt plays a poor-quality cassette tape for Saunders that he says was recorded by the four men involved in the potential assault. According to Eckardt, one of the plotters on the tape asks, "Why don't we just kill her?" Eckardt says that's unnecessary, directs men to "just hit her in the knee."

January 3

Unable to assault Kerrigan on Cape Cod, Stant takes a bus to Detroit, site of the nationals.

Another $3,000 is withdrawn by Gillooly from his account.

January 4

Stant arrives in the Detroit suburb of Romulus, Michigan.

January 5

A phone call is made from Stant's motel room to the Gillooly/Harding residence. Eckardt wires $750 to Derrick Smith and Smith flies from Phoenix to Detroit.

January 6

Once again, Gillooly withdraws $3,000 from his Portland account. Eckardt sends $1,300, via Western Union, to Smith.

Stant attacks Kerrigan at Cobo Arena, Detroit.

January 7

Stant and Smith fly to Phoenix.

Kerrigan withdraws from the nationals due to the injury suffered in the assault.

January 8

Harding finishes first at the nationals; 13-year-old Michelle Kwan is second.

An unidentified woman telephones Detroit police and names Gillooly, Eckardt, Smith and Stant as four men whom she heard on an audio tape planning to hurt Kerrigan. This is the first break in the case.

January 10

Harding flies back to Portland and reveals that Michigan police have questioned her about the Kerrigan assault. She asserts she had no involvement in the case.

Eugene Saunders, Eckardt's classmate, informs the FBI of his conversation with the bodyguard.

The FBI question Eckardt for the first time.

January 12

Eckardt signs a confession. He also names Gillooly, Stant and Smith.

January 13

Eckardt and Smith are arrested and charged with conspiracy to commit second-degree assault. Newspaper reports break the story that the authorities consider Gillooly a suspect in the case.

January 14

The FBI arrest Stant in Phoenix; he signs a confession implicating Gillooly, Eckardt and Smith.

Portland law enforcement officials deny that Harding herself would be arrested.

January 16

Kerrigan returns to the ice for the first time.

Amid swirling rumors, Harding denies any involvement in the Kerrigan attack.

January 18

For the first time, Harding is questioned by the FBI in a ten-hour session. Through an attorney, Harding says she is splitting from Gillooly to concentrate on her skating.

Stant, returned to Portland, is charged with conspiracy and assault.

January 19

Gillooly is arrested; also charged with conspiracy and assault.

In an explosive newspaper interview, Eckardt claims Harding was part of the plot on Kerrigan.

January 20

Harding skates in public for the first time since the assault on Kerrigan. She performs beautifully, landing several triple Axels.

Friends of Harding and Gillooly testify before a Multnomah County grand jury.

January 21

The deadline for the grand jury report is pushed back to February 3.

Skating at home in Stoneham, Massachusetts, Kerrigan lands her first triple jumps since the attack. After the session, she declines to answer questions from reporters. Later in the day she flies to Los Angeles to film a television commercial.

At the Clackamas Town Center rink, more than 400 fans and supporters, many wearing "We Believe in Tonya" buttons, watch Harding skate.

January 23

The Portland *Oregonian* runs a story in which Harding is accused by two men of trying to have Gillooly killed the previous summer. An unnamed source says an angry Harding approached the men and told them she wanted Gillooly "taken care of."

January 25

Reports surface for the first time that Gillooly has implicated Harding in exchange for a lighter sentence.

The deadline for the grand jury report is pushed back again, this time to February 18, six days after the start of the Winter Olympics.

January 26

Gillooly and his attorney, Ron Hoevet, meet with authorities for more than six hours.

January 28

A Detroit television station reports that it has obtained phone records showing that ten phone calls to Shawn Eckardt's home were charged to Harding's personal telephone credit card on January 4 and again on January 6, the day Kerrigan was assaulted.

The station also reports that an employee at the Detroit Westin Hotel—where most competitors stayed during the national championships—told investigators Harding had asked for Kerrigan's room number.

January 29

The New York Times reports that Gillooly has reached an agreement with prosecutors. Under the terms of the plea bargain, prosecutors would charge Gillooly with a single count of racketeering and seek a maximum sentence of two years in prison.

John Gillooly tells the New York *Daily News* that his brother did in fact implicate Tonya Harding during the course of his interrogation by the FBI—but only after discovering that Harding had "double-crossed" him.

Gillooly shows up at the home of Shawn Eckardt and begins pounding on the front door. Police are summoned to the scene, and Gillooly leaves without incident.

January 30

Gillooly's attorney, Ron Hoevet, says his client will probably hold a press conference within a few days.

January 31

Rosters for the Winter Olympic Games are submitted. Tonya Harding's name is included.

January 31

Philip Knight, Chief Executive Officer of NIKE, announces that his company will contribute $25,000 to help Harding defend herself if the U.S. Olympic Committee attempts to remove her from the team.

February 1

Jeff Gillooly enters into a plea agreement with the Multnomah County District Attorney's office, in which he pleads guilty to one count of "racketeering" in exchange for a reduced sentence and an agreement to testify "truly and fully" in the Nancy Kerrigan assault case. In a statement read by his lawyer, Ron Hoevet, Gillooly, for the first time, formally alleges that Tonya Harding was involved in the plot.

Hoevet also urges Harding to admit her role in the plot. "Denial is no longer plausible," Hoevet said. "The truth about this bizarre crime has now been revealed." In a press conference later, Hoevet added, "She did much more than know about it, she actively participated in it."

Harding's reaction to Gillooly's accusations is one of complete and utter denial. Her lawyer, Robert Weaver, said, after Hoevet's press conference: "Tonya Harding denies the accusations leveled against her by her former husband and boyfriend, Jeff Gillooly. . . . I am appalled that Mr. Gillooly's attorney has seen fit to immerse himself in this media circus . . . It is my hope that charges will not be leveled against Tonya Harding . . . If charges are leveled against her, she will respond to them in a court of law."

Appendix B

COMPETITIVE HISTORY HIGHLIGHTS

1994 National Senior — 1st
1993 National Senior — 4th
1992 World Championships — 6th
1992 Olympic Winter Games — 4th
1992 National Senior — 3rd
1991 Skate America — 1st
1991 World Championships — 2nd
1991 National Senior — 1st
1990 NHK Trophy — 2nd
1990 Olympic Festival — 2nd
1990 National Senior — 7th
1989 Nations Cup — 1st
1989 Skate America — 1st
1989 National Senior — 3rd
1988 Prize of Moscow News — 1st
1988 National Senior — 5th
1987 NHK Trophy — 3rd
1987 La Coupe Excellence — 1st
1987 National Senior — 5th

1986 Skate America — 2nd
1986 Olympic Festival — 3rd
1986 National Senior — 6th
1985 Olympic Festival — 5th
1984 National Junior — 6th

Appendix C

NOTABLE QUOTATIONS ON THE HARDING/KERRIGAN AFFAIR

"I haven't done anything wrong."

—Tonya Harding

"Legally, Harding has the right to skate in Lillehammer. But she shouldn't be there. She and her associates are an embarrassment to this country and an embarrassment to the standards of sportsmanship and fair play."

—Dan Shaughnessy
The Boston Globe

"Tonya Harding is not a murderer, nor is she a criminal, nor is she an accomplice to a crime. . . . In the eyes of the law, Tonya Harding is innocent. Believe me, the FBI and the Multnomah County district attorney's office would be happy to add her shiny blonde scalp to their collection."

—Alex Beam
The Boston Globe

"This is not a beyond-reasonable-doubt-type prosecution. Obviously some subjective judgments will have to be made on what is sportsmanship. But there is also a lot of objective material."

—William Hybl
Chairman, USFSA investigative panel

"Tonya Harding proves that you don't have to be a Barbie doll to succeed in this sport. Tonya certainly is *not* a Barbie doll. She's a fighter."

—Michael Rosenberg
Harding's former agent

"As they say around Tonya Harding's hometown of Portland, Oregon: 'TIM-berr!' She has cut herself down. She has cleared herself from the Olympic forest. . . ."

—John Jeansonne
Newsday

"I am embarrassed and ashamed that anyone close to me would be involved."

—Tonya Harding

"I had no prior knowledge on the planned assault on Nancy Kerrigan."

—Tonya Harding

"I am responsible, however, for failing to report things I learned about the assault when I returned home from nationals."

—Tonya Harding

"She (Tonya) wouldn't even hurt a fly if she couldn't help it. She was never vicious."

—LaVona (Harding) Golden
Tonya's mother

"I've seen her mother slap her and knock her off a chair."

—Pat Hammill
whose daughter competed with Harding

"What a bitch."

—Tonya Harding
(at age 15, on her mother)

"She (Tonya) wouldn't jeopardize her career like that."

—James Golden
Tonya's stepfather

"She's a very driven girl, but I don't think she's capable of anything like that (the attack). Even if she's as innocent as the driven snow, this will affect her reputation forever, and it's very sad."
—JoJo Starbuck
Professional figure skater

"She'll never have her sponsors. Not the way the media has destroyed her."
—LaVona Golden

"Not much anymore. It breaks my heart to say that."
—LaVona Golden
on the gold medal's worth to Harding

"To be honest, going to jail will be good for Jeff. At least they'll give him three squares, a roof over his head and maybe some training. And he can't go back to Tonya."
—John Gillooly
brother of Jeff Gillooly

"Perhaps Kerrigan can defeat Tonya in accounting rooms in tournaments, with media favoritism and Eastern seaboard hype, but she will never defeat Tonya on the ice, at figure skating."
—Team Tonya fan club newsletter
(excerpt from unsigned article)

"We're not so cut-throat as a sport that we don't recognize the right thing to do."

—Carol Heiss Jenkins
coach of the Kerrigan/Harding
competitors, on the decision to name
Kerrigan to the Olympic team

"We might not like what she did, and we might think it is bad judgment, but it is not a crime unless there is some affirmative act on her part to conceal, to harbor someone in flight, to accept money for not talking."

—Robert Goffredi
Portland criminal lawyer, explaining
why Harding's admission of withholding
information about the Kerrigan case
was not a criminal act in Oregon

"She's guiltier than hell."

—James Golden
Harding's estranged stepfather

"Please believe in me."

—Tonya Harding

Appendix D

Excerpts from the United States Figure Skating Association's Code of Conduct (which Tonya Harding signed prior to competing in the Nationals in Detroit in December):

"I will exemplify the highest standards of fairness, ethical behavior, and genuine good sportsmanship in all my relations with others."

"I understand that if my acts, statements, or conduct are considered detrimental to the welfare of figure skating by the appropriate authority, I may be subject to penalties imposed by the USFSA (United States Figure Skating Association)."

"I understand that the penalties that may be imposed may include, but are not limited to, loss of future international selections and loss of participations in USFSA-sponsored events."

"Any person whose acts, statements or conduct is considered detrimental to the welfare of figure skating is subject to loss of the privilege of registration by the USFSA . . . loss of membership privileges, suspension and expulsion."

Members of the United States Figure Skating Association's Investigative Panel (whose recommendation to the USFSA will likely be decisive in determining whether Tonya Harding will compete in the Olympic Games):

WILLIAM HYBL, CHAIRMAN: Former interim president of the United States Olympic Committee; former special White House counsel serving under Ronald Reagan; current president of the El Pomar corporation.

COL. KEN SCHWEITZER: Athletic director of the United States Air Force Academy.

DR. NANCY PIRO: Chairman of the USFSA Ethics Committee.

DR. SHARON WATSON: Executive Director of the Los Angeles Children's Planning Council.

JIM CYSAN: A former figure skater, now a medical student, who will serve as "athlete representative" for the panel.

Appendix E

Organizations with jurisdictional responsibilities in the Tonya Harding case:

The United States Figure Skating Association
   (USFSA)
20 First Street, Colorado Springs, CO 80906
(719) 635-5200
President: Claire Ferguson

The United States Olympic Committee (USOC)
1750 East Boulder St., Colorado Springs, CO
   80909
(719) 578-4529
Executive Director: Harvey Schiller

International Olympic Committee (IOC)
Chateau de Vidy, CH 1007 Lausanne, Switzerland
Tel: 011-41-21-253-271
President: Juan Antonio Samaranch